HISTORY OF J
FUSION OF TRADITION, CULTURE, AND
OLYMPIC SUCCESS

How Traditional Bökh Wrestling Shaped Mongolia's Judo Champions

By

Leighton Tokunbo Shepherd

Copyright Page

History of Judo in Mongolia: A Fusion of Tradition, Culture, and Olympic Success

Book Description

Mongolia has a profound and ancient connection to wrestling, known as Bökh in the local language. Wrestling transcends mere sport in Mongolia; it embodies a longstanding tradition dating back to the era of nomadic warriors. It serves as a dual purpose, testing both strength and skill, essential not only in festivities but also in historical battle contexts. Wrestling is deeply ingrained in Mongolia's culture, functioning not just for entertainment but as a core aspect of life. It imparts essential values like discipline, resilience, and honor, perpetuated through generations.The introduction of Judo, a modern martial art from Japan, to Mongolia in the mid-20th century initially appeared foreign and rigid compared to the dynamic and unpredictable Bökh style. Initially viewed as an intriguing novelty, Judo gradually found resonance within Mongolian culture. The underlying philosophy of Judo emphasizing respect, balance, and mental fortitude aligned seamlessly with Mongolia's cultural ethos. Many Mongolian wrestlers found a sense of familiarity in Judo techniques, recognizing them as variations of their traditional practices honed over centuries on the Mongolian steppes.

What ensued was a striking amalgamation of tradition and innovation. Mongolian athletes melded their ancient Bökh skills with the principles of Judo, culminating in a distinctive style that harmonized the vigor of traditional wrestling with the finesse and tactics of modern Judo. This fusion propelled Mongolian Judo practitioners onto the global arena, where their throws stood out for their unpredictability, explosiveness, and difficulty to counter. They engaged not only physically but also with an intense pride, embodying the spirit of their forebears in every competition.This narrative chronicles the evolution of Mongolia's age-old wrestling customs into contemporary Judo triumphs. It delves into the cultural and historical foundations of Bökh, illustrating how wrestling held a pivotal role in the lives of nomadic societies. Beyond a mere sport, wrestling symbolized rites of passage, conflict resolution, and a tribute to strength and resilience. It was a preparation for life's adversities, embodying a way of existence. As Judo expanded globally, Mongolia's wrestlers swiftly emerged as formidable contenders. Despite resource constraints, they adeptly adapted to the sport's regulations, leveraging their distinctive background to surprise and overpower more seasoned adversaries.

The book illuminates Mongolia's journey in international Judo competitions, from modest origins to significant triumphs. It underscores how Mongolia's traditional approach to Judo has distinguished them as one of the most esteemed and enigmatic teams in the discipline. The narrative further delves into the obstacles encountered by Mongolian athletes, who often trained under austere conditions with minimal access to advanced training facilities. Their relentless spirit persevered despite grappling on dusty terrain with rudimentary equipment. Rooted in their wrestling legacy, their training emphasized equilibrium, footwork, and forceful throws. While other nations adhered to conventional Judo methods, Mongolian fighters brought forth an untamed, inventive style that kept opponents on edge.This account underscores how Judo transcended mere sport in Mongolia, assuming the role of a national emblem and a means for a modest nation to assert its presence on the global stage. Judo now signifies a link between Mongolia's past and future, honoring ancient customs while attaining contemporary success. Each throw, each victory, pays homage to Mongolia's wrestling heritage. The uniqueness of Mongolian Judo lies not solely in the accolades or titles but in the narratives that accompany these achievements. Stories of athletes training in makeshift facilities, embarking on arduous journeys for competitions, and confronting not just adversaries but also poverty, harsh environments, and cultural expectations. Their voyage epitomizes resilience, creativity, and pride in their lineage.

Additionally, the narrative explores the distinctive techniques that differentiate Mongolian Judo. It elucidates how adapting traditional Bökh maneuvers to Judo regulations provided Mongolian fighters with a competitive advantage in international settings. Unlike their counterparts, Mongolia's Judokas do not conform to the conventional patterns of formal Judo. Instead, they rely on instinct and improvisation, drawing from moves refined over centuries of wrestling in Mongolia's rugged, expansive landscapes.This is more than a tale of Judo; it encapsulates the essence of a nation's spirit.

portraying how a populace with a resolute, warrior ethos embraced an unfamiliar martial art and made it their own. It epitomizes the integration of ancient traditions with contemporary methodologies and the evolution of tradition while preserving its core.

From the windswept steppes to the grand stages of international contests, this narrative traces Mongolia's ascent in the realm of Judo while honoring its origins. Through vivid historical narratives, intricate technique analyses, and accounts of athletes' tenacity, this book provides an insightful exploration of the cultural amalgamation that defines Mongolian Judo. It celebrates strength, perseverance, and the enduring link between tradition and advancement.

table of Contents

Introduction

Wrestling is one of the oldest forms of combat in human history. Long before professional wrestling became a spectacle in arenas, the act of grappling was deeply tied to survival, honor, and even spirituality. It wasn't about showmanship or flashy moves—it was a practical skill for warriors, hunters, and even leaders.

Ancient cultures all over the world had their own versions of wrestling. In Greece, there was **pankration**, a mix of wrestling and striking that became part of the early Olympic Games. The Greeks saw wrestling as a way to build not only physical strength but also character. In their mythology, even the gods wrestled. Zeus himself was said to have defeated the mighty Titan Cronus through wrestling, symbolizing the power of cunning and skill over brute force.

Across the sea, the Egyptians had their own style of wrestling. Ancient tomb paintings dating back thousands of years show men locked in grappling positions that look very familiar to modern wrestling fans. In those days, wrestling was part of military training. It wasn't just a sport; it was a tool for survival on the battlefield. The better you were at wrestling, the better your chances of walking away from a fight alive.

In Japan, **sumo wrestling** has roots that stretch back over a thousand years. But sumo wasn't always the ceremonial sport it is today. It began as a rougher, more brutal form of combat used to please the gods during religious festivals. The ring—known as the **dohyō—is** considered sacred, and the rituals around sumo are meant to honor tradition and spirituality. Even today, sumo wrestlers are seen as cultural icons in Japan, with a strict code of conduct that traces back to ancient customs.

Let's not forget **India's kushti wrestling**, practiced in mud pits rather than mats. Kushti dates back to the **Malla-yuddha** tradition, which is mentioned in ancient texts. Wrestlers in this style follow strict diets and training routines, treating the art as both a physical and spiritual practice. A wrestler isn't just someone who fights—he's expected to be disciplined, humble, and dedicated to his craft.

In more recent history, wrestling became popular in Europe during the medieval period. Knights would often engage in grappling to improve their close-combat skills. Unlike sword fights, wrestling taught warriors how to handle themselves when they were disarmed or thrown to the ground. The Germans had a term for this: **ringen**, which referred to a form of grappling practiced both as a sport and a battlefield technique. There's even a famous 15th-century German manual on wrestling by a man named **Fiore dei Liberi**, which shows detailed drawings of holds, throws, and counters.

Meanwhile, in the British Isles, folk wrestling styles emerged.

For example, **Cornish wrestling** has been practiced for centuries in England. The wrestlers wore jackets, and the goal was to throw the opponent onto the ground with both shoulders touching. Similarly, **collar-and-elbow wrestling** became popular in Ireland. This style influenced early forms of American wrestling after Irish immigrants brought it to the United States.

Wrestling also found its way into Native American cultures. Tribes used wrestling to teach young warriors endurance, strength, and strategy. These matches weren't just about winning — they were a way to build resilience and mental toughness, traits essential for survival in harsh conditions.

In the 19th and early 20th centuries, wrestling began to evolve into more of a sport than a survival skill. **Catch wrestling** emerged in England and quickly spread to the United States. This style combined grappling and submission holds. It was called "catch-as-catch-can" because wrestlers could grab any part of their opponent's body to gain control. Catch wrestling is the foundation of modern professional wrestling and has heavily influenced other combat sports like MMA (mixed martial arts).

American wrestling grew even more popular in the late 1800s. Traveling carnivals featured wrestling matches where locals could challenge a "strongman" wrestler for a cash prize. These matches weren't always legitimate — promoters would often stage the outcomes to ensure the house wrestler won. Over time, this led to the rise of **professional wrestling**, with scripted matches and colorful characters. But even with the theatrics, the core of wrestling remained the same: grappling, throws, and holds.

Today, wrestling is divided into different styles. **Freestyle wrestling** and **Greco-Roman wrestling** are the two main forms seen in the Olympics. Freestyle allows wrestlers to use their legs for both offense and defense, while Greco-Roman focuses solely on upper-body techniques. Both styles require incredible strength, balance, and technique, with matches often won by pinning an opponent or scoring points through takedowns and throws.

In addition to these Olympic styles, there's **collegiate wrestling** in the United States, also known as **folkstyle wrestling**. It's the style practiced in high schools and colleges across the country. This type of wrestling emphasizes control, with points awarded for maintaining dominant positions and escaping from holds.

Outside of traditional and competitive wrestling, we also have **pro wrestling**, which combines athleticism with entertainment. While it's scripted, the physical demands on wrestlers are real. They perform night after night, putting their bodies on the line in matches that require precision and timing to avoid serious injury. Organizations like **WWE** have made pro wrestling a global phenomenon, blending storytelling with athletic performances.

It's worth noting that wrestling techniques have also influenced other combat sports. **Judo**, for example, focuses on throws and takedowns, similar to wrestling. In judo, the goal is to use your opponent's momentum against them, a concept that's shared across many wrestling styles. **Brazilian jiu-jitsu** (BJJ) has its roots in judo and incorporates a lot of wrestling-style submissions and control techniques. BJJ practitioners often train to dominate their opponents on the ground through grappling and positional control.

Even modern mixed martial arts wouldn't be what it is today without wrestling. Many of the best fighters in **UFC** history have a wrestling background. Wrestling gives fighters a solid base in controlling their opponents, dictating where the fight goes, and defending against submissions. In MMA, the ability to take someone down and keep them there can be the difference between winning and losing.

So, when we talk about wrestling, we're really talking about one of the most ancient and enduring forms of human combat. It's evolved over thousands of years, from tribal rituals and battlefield techniques to Olympic sports and entertainment spectacles. But at its core, wrestling remains about two people testing their strength, skill, and willpower. It's one of the purest forms of competition — no weapons, no tricks, just one person against another, trying to prove who's stronger and more skilled.

And that's why wrestling, in all its forms, has stood the test of time. It's not just about the throws or the techniques. It's about discipline, endurance, and the timeless struggle of man against man.

Chapter 1: Wrestling in the Time of Genghis Khan

The Role of Bökh Wrestling in Mongolian Society During the Mongol Empire

Wrestling played a central role in the Mongol Empire, especially under the leadership of Genghis Khan. The Mongolian style of wrestling, known as **Bökh**, wasn't just a sport. It was a way of life, deeply embedded in Mongolian culture, tradition, and even politics. The word "Bökh" itself means **"strong" or "durable"**, which shows how highly physical strength and endurance were valued in Mongolian society.

During the time of Genghis Khan, Bökh wrestling was a way to prove your worth, both as a warrior and as a man. Strength and skill in wrestling weren't just for show — they were practical tools for survival in a harsh, nomadic lifestyle. Mongolian tribes lived on the steppe, a vast, open grassland with extreme weather conditions. Life there was tough, and the ability to fight, hunt, and protect your family was essential.

Genghis Khan himself was said to be a skilled wrestler. Legends say he used his wrestling skills to defeat rivals during his rise to power. In Mongolian tradition, wrestling wasn't about size or brute strength alone. It was about technique, strategy, and mental toughness. A smaller wrestler could defeat a larger opponent through superior skill, a concept that reflected Genghis Khan's own rise from humble beginnings to become the ruler of the largest land empire in history.

Bökh and Warrior Culture

In Mongolian society, wrestling was more than a sport; it was part of military training. Warriors practiced Bökh to build strength, agility, and endurance. Wrestling taught them how to handle themselves in close combat, a skill that was essential on the battlefield.

Mongol warriors were known for their **hit-and-run tactics** and their ability to fight on horseback, but when it came to hand-to-hand combat, Bökh wrestling techniques came into play. If a warrior was unhorsed in battle, his wrestling skills could mean the difference between life and death.

Unlike modern wrestling styles, Bökh doesn't involve pins or submissions. The goal is simple: to throw your opponent to the ground. If any part of their body other than their feet touches the ground, you win. This emphasis on throws and balance made Bökh practical for real-world combat situations. Mongolian wrestlers learned how to use their opponents' momentum against them, a skill that translated well to battlefield tactics.

Wrestling as a Social Hierarchy Tool

During Genghis Khan's reign, wrestling wasn't just about physical strength — it was also a way to gain **status and respect** within the community. Wrestling tournaments were often held at major gatherings, including weddings, religious festivals, and military campaigns.

Victory in wrestling brought **prestige and honor**. A strong wrestler could gain the attention of tribal leaders, receive rewards, and even rise in social rank. For a nomad living on the steppe, being a successful wrestler could open doors to opportunities that wouldn't be available otherwise.

Genghis Khan understood the importance of this. He encouraged wrestling tournaments at **Naadam**, a traditional festival that included three main sports: **wrestling, horse racing, and archery**. These were known as the **"Three Manly Skills"**, essential for any Mongolian man who aspired to be a warrior. Wrestling was the most prestigious event at Naadam and remains so to this day.

The Wrestling Outfit

One unique aspect of Bökh wrestling is the **traditional outfit** worn by the wrestlers. They wear a jacket called a **zodog** and shorts known as **shuudag**. The design of the outfit has an interesting story behind it.

According to legend, a female wrestler once entered a tournament disguised as a man and defeated several opponents. To prevent this from happening again, the traditional zodog was modified to leave the chest area bare, ensuring that only men could compete. This story shows how deeply ingrained wrestling was in Mongolian ideas of masculinity and warrior culture.

Genghis Khan's Wrestling Code

Genghis Khan wasn't just a military genius — he was also a visionary leader who created a legal code known as the **Yassa**. This code governed many aspects of Mongolian life, including wrestling.

Under the Yassa, wrestling matches had strict rules to prevent cheating or dishonorable behavior. For example, a wrestler couldn't strike or harm their opponent outside the agreed rules. The matches were expected to be fair and respectful. These values reflected the Mongol warrior code of **honor and loyalty**.

Genghis Khan believed that discipline and respect in wrestling mirrored the qualities he wanted in his soldiers. His armies were successful not only because of their tactics but also because of their discipline and loyalty to their leader. Wrestling reinforced these values.

Wrestling as a Unifying Force

One of Genghis Khan's greatest achievements was **uniting the Mongol tribes**, which had been divided by conflicts and rivalries for centuries. Wrestling played a role in this unification.

When Genghis Khan brought different tribes together, he often held wrestling tournaments as part of the celebrations. These matches helped ease tensions between rival groups. Wrestling became a **symbol of unity**, showing that while tribes might have different customs, they all respected the art of Bökh.

This tradition continued even after Genghis Khan's death. His successors, including **Kublai Khan**, promoted wrestling as part of Mongolian culture. Wrestling remained an important way to build camaraderie among soldiers and to celebrate important events.

The Legacy of Bökh

Today, Bökh remains a **national sport** in Mongolia. The Naadam festival is still celebrated every year, with wrestling as the main event. Modern Bökh tournaments have hundreds of participants, and the winners are given titles like **"Champion of Mongolia"** or **"Titan"**.

The techniques and traditions of Bökh have also influenced other combat sports around the world. The emphasis on balance, throws, and using an opponent's momentum can be seen in **judo**, **sambo**, and even **MMA**.

But for Mongolians, Bökh is more than just a sport. It's a link to their history, a reminder of the days when Genghis Khan and his warriors rode across the steppe, conquering vast territories. Wrestling symbolizes **strength, unity, and resilience**, traits that have defined Mongolian culture for centuries.

In the time of Genghis Khan, wrestling was more than entertainment. It was a way to prove yourself, to rise through the ranks, and to prepare for the harsh realities of life on the steppe. For the Mongols, wrestling wasn't just a game — it was a reflection of their warrior spirit.

Wrestling Tournaments: Building Strength, Unity, and Discipline in the Mongol Army

During the rise of the Mongol Empire, wrestling tournaments were more than just sporting events — they were tools used to shape the mindset and abilities of Genghis Khan's warriors. Wrestling, known as **Bökh**, played a key role in preparing soldiers for the harsh demands of war. These tournaments helped build physical strength, foster unity among the troops, and instill a sense of discipline that was essential for maintaining order in one of history's most formidable armies.

Strength Through Wrestling

For Mongol soldiers, strength wasn't just measured by how hard you could swing a weapon. It was about endurance, balance, and control — all qualities that wrestling develops. The harsh conditions of life on the steppe meant that physical toughness was a requirement for survival, and wrestling provided a practical way to build that toughness.

Wrestling tournaments were used as part of regular military training. Soldiers would grapple with one another to improve their stamina, learn how to control an opponent, and develop the ability to stay calm under pressure. These skills translated directly to the battlefield. Wrestling taught warriors how to take an enemy to the ground quickly and effectively, which was especially important when disarmed or fighting at close range.

Unlike some forms of combat training that focused solely on weapon use, wrestling prepared soldiers for situations where brute strength alone wouldn't win the fight. It emphasized **leverage, technique, and timing**, teaching soldiers how to defeat stronger or larger opponents by using their momentum against them.

Wrestling also helped improve **core strength and flexibility**, critical for handling the heavy armor and weapons used in battle. A soldier who could endure a long wrestling match was more likely to endure the grueling marches and long campaigns that characterized Mongol warfare.

Unity Among the Troops

One of Genghis Khan's greatest challenges was uniting the various Mongol tribes, many of which had long histories of conflict with one another. Wrestling tournaments provided a way to ease tensions between these groups and build camaraderie among the troops.

When soldiers from different tribes competed in wrestling matches, it created a sense of shared identity. Even if they came from rival clans, the soldiers were bound by the same traditions and values. Wrestling became a **symbol of unity**, reminding everyone that they were part of something bigger than their individual tribes — they were part of Genghis Khan's army.

Tournaments also gave soldiers a chance to earn respect based on merit rather than birth or tribal affiliation. In wrestling, social status didn't matter. What mattered was strength, skill, and perseverance. This merit-based recognition helped break down barriers between tribes and fostered loyalty to the larger Mongol cause.

Wrestling matches were often held at **military gatherings and celebrations**, where soldiers could bond with one another outside the context of battle. These gatherings strengthened the sense of brotherhood among the troops and reduced internal conflicts that might have weakened the army.

Discipline Through Competition

Discipline was a cornerstone of Genghis Khan's success. His army wasn't the largest in the world, but it was one of the most organized and efficient. Wrestling tournaments helped enforce the discipline that kept the Mongol forces in line.

First, the rules of wrestling taught soldiers to respect boundaries and follow a code of conduct. In traditional Bökh matches, there were clear rules about what was allowed and what wasn't. For example, striking or using dirty tactics was forbidden. Soldiers learned to fight honorably, even in high-pressure situations.

Second, wrestling taught soldiers how to handle **defeat** without losing morale. In battle, not every encounter ends in victory. A soldier who could lose a wrestling match, shake hands with his opponent, and come back stronger for the next round was better prepared for the ups and downs of war. Wrestling tournaments fostered **mental resilience**, which was just as important as physical toughness.

Third, the tournaments encouraged **consistency in training**. To compete in wrestling matches, soldiers needed to maintain their fitness levels and stay sharp. This regular training routine kept the troops battle-ready, even during times of peace. Wrestling wasn't just a once-in-a-while event — it was part of the soldiers' everyday lives.

Genghis Khan valued discipline in every aspect of his army. Soldiers were expected to follow orders without hesitation, and wrestling taught them to control their impulses and think strategically. In a wrestling match, rushing in without a plan often leads to defeat. The same principle applied on the battlefield. Wrestling helped soldiers develop **patience, focus, and tactical thinking** — all of which were vital for executing complex military maneuvers.

A Tool for Identifying Leaders

Wrestling tournaments also served as a way to **identify promising leaders** within the ranks. In Mongolian culture, wrestling success was a sign of more than just physical ability. It indicated **mental toughness, courage, and determination** — qualities that Genghis Khan valued in his commanders.

Winning a wrestling match required **quick thinking and adaptability**, traits that were just as important in battle. A soldier who could outmaneuver an opponent in a wrestling ring was likely to be just as resourceful on the battlefield.

Genghis Khan reportedly promoted soldiers based on merit rather than family ties or social status. Wrestling tournaments gave him a chance to see who had the potential to rise through the ranks. Those who demonstrated skill, determination, and leadership in the wrestling ring were often given greater responsibilities within the army.

Boosting Morale and Celebrating Victories

In addition to their practical benefits, wrestling tournaments also served a **cultural and morale-boosting function**. After a successful campaign, wrestling matches were held as part of victory celebrations. These events gave soldiers a chance to unwind and showcase their skills in front of their comrades.

The tournaments provided a sense of **normalcy and tradition** in the midst of war. No matter how far the Mongol army traveled or how many battles they fought, wrestling remained a familiar part of their lives. It reminded soldiers of home and reinforced the values they had been taught since childhood.

For Genghis Khan, these celebrations were a way to reward his soldiers and **keep morale high**. Wrestling wasn't just about competition; it was about **honoring tradition and building a sense of pride** in being part of the Mongol army.

Legacy in Modern Military Training

The use of wrestling as a military training tool didn't end with the Mongol Empire. Many modern armies incorporate grappling and hand-to-hand combat training in their routines.

The principles of wrestling — strength, balance, discipline, and adaptability — are still valuable in today's military forces.

The Mongol Empire's success wasn't just about tactics or numbers. It was about the **discipline, unity, and strength** of its soldiers. Wrestling tournaments played a key role in shaping those qualities. By promoting fitness, camaraderie, and mental toughness, wrestling helped Genghis Khan create an army that was not only powerful but also cohesive and resilient.

In the end, wrestling wasn't just a sport for the Mongols — it was a way to prepare for war, build loyalty, and ensure the long-term success of the empire.

Chapter 2: Bökh Wrestling and Nomadic Culture

Bökh as a Reflection of Nomadic Values

The nomadic lifestyle of the Mongols revolved around **mobility and self-reliance**. Families moved across vast landscapes, following herds of livestock and adapting to the seasons. In such an environment, wrestling served as a critical way to prepare young men for the demands of life on the steppe.

Bökh wrestling wasn't just about proving who was the strongest. It was seen as a way to **build character** and teach important life lessons. Wrestlers were expected to show **honor, humility, and respect** toward their opponents, values that mirrored the behavior expected in daily life. A successful wrestler was not only physically strong but also mentally disciplined and morally upright.

In nomadic society, these traits were essential. Life on the steppe was harsh and unforgiving, with harsh winters, scarce resources, and the constant threat of raids from rival tribes. Wrestling helped instill the physical and mental toughness needed to survive in such an environment.

The Spiritual Aspect of Bökh

Bökh also had a spiritual dimension. The Mongols believed in **Tengrism**, a belief system centered around **Tengri**, the eternal sky god. For the Mongols, nature and the spiritual world were deeply intertwined, and wrestling was seen as a way to honor the spirits.

Wrestling matches were often accompanied by **rituals and ceremonies** to show respect to the spirits of the land and the ancestors. The wrestling ring, or **dohyo**, was considered a sacred space, representing the balance between heaven and earth. Before entering the ring, wrestlers would perform a traditional **"eagle dance"** to honor the sky god. This dance, with its sweeping arm movements, symbolized strength, freedom, and a connection to nature.

Winning a wrestling match wasn't just a personal achievement — it was seen as a **blessing from the spirits**. Wrestlers who performed well were believed to have received the favor of Tengri, making them respected figures in their communities.

Wrestling as a Rite of Passage

In Mongolian nomadic culture, Bökh wrestling was also a **rite of passage** for young men. Boys would begin wrestling at a young age, learning the techniques and traditions from their elders. Competing in wrestling matches was a way to prove their **readiness for adulthood** and gain respect within the tribe.

Winning a match wasn't just about physical prowess. It demonstrated that the young man was capable of handling himself in difficult situations and could be trusted to protect his family and contribute to the tribe's well-being.

Wrestling tournaments were often held during important life events, such as **weddings, births, and festivals**. These events brought the entire community together and reinforced social bonds. A wrestling victory at one of these gatherings was seen as a sign that the winner would have **good fortune and success** in life.

The Symbolism of Strength and Balance

In Bökh wrestling, strength is important, but it's not the only factor that determines success. The sport places a heavy emphasis on **balance, agility, and technique**. A skilled wrestler must know how to **use an opponent's momentum against them**, staying calm and strategic even in high-pressure situations.

This focus on balance reflects a key aspect of nomadic life. The Mongols had to constantly balance their lives with the forces of nature, adapting to changing conditions and making the most of limited resources. Wrestling taught them to stay grounded, both literally and figuratively.

In a spiritual sense, balance also represented the **harmony between heaven and earth**, a core belief in Tengrism. The best wrestlers were those who could maintain this harmony — staying rooted in tradition while adapting to the challenges in front of them.

A Celebration of Community and Tradition

Bökh wrestling wasn't just a sport for individuals; it was a **community event** that brought people together. Wrestling tournaments were often held during **Naadam**, a traditional festival that celebrates the "three manly skills" of wrestling, horse racing, and archery. Naadam is one of the most important cultural events in Mongolia, and it dates back to the time of the Mongol Empire.

During Naadam, wrestling wasn't just about competition. It was a way to **honor the ancestors, celebrate unity, and preserve cultural traditions**. The festival emphasized the importance of community, reminding people that they were part of something greater than themselves.

Even today, wrestling at Naadam is deeply rooted in tradition. Wrestlers wear the **zodog** (a sleeveless jacket) and **shuudag** (shorts), and matches are accompanied by ceremonial music and dances. The rituals have remained largely unchanged for centuries, a testament to the enduring significance of wrestling in Mongolian culture.

The Role of Wrestling in Family Life

In nomadic families, wrestling wasn't just for competition — it was a **part of daily life**. Fathers would teach their sons how to wrestle as a way to **pass down knowledge and tradition**. Wrestling matches between family members were common, and they helped strengthen familial bonds.

These family wrestling sessions weren't always serious competitions. They were often seen as **playful and educational**, teaching children about resilience, respect, and perseverance. Even today, Mongolian families continue this tradition, with young boys learning to wrestle from their elders.

Wrestling also played a role in **storytelling and folklore**. Many Mongolian legends feature stories of great wrestlers who used their strength and skill to achieve heroic deeds. These stories were passed down through generations, reinforcing the cultural importance of Bökh.

A Lasting Cultural Legacy

The cultural and spiritual significance of Bökh continues to shape Mongolian identity today. Wrestling is more than just a sport — it's a **symbol of resilience, strength, and tradition**. The techniques, rituals, and values associated with Bökh have been passed down for generations, keeping the nomadic spirit alive in modern Mongolia.

Even as Mongolia has become more urbanized, wrestling remains a key part of national identity. The Naadam festival continues to be celebrated every year, with thousands of wrestlers competing in matches that honor their cultural heritage. Bökh wrestling has also gained recognition outside of Mongolia, with international tournaments showcasing this ancient tradition to the world.

For Mongolians, Bökh is a **living connection to their ancestors**. It's a reminder of the nomadic way of life, the challenges of the steppe, and the values that have sustained their people for centuries. In a world that is constantly changing, Bökh remains a constant — a testament to the strength and resilience of the Mongolian spirit.

Wrestling as a Rite of Passage for Young Boys and a Symbol of Masculinity and Honor

Wrestling in Mongolian culture wasn't just a game for boys to pass the time. It was serious business. From the time they could walk, boys were taught to wrestle. This wasn't about showing off or playing around — it was about **becoming a man**. Wrestling was one of the first tests a boy had to face to prove he was ready to take on the responsibilities of adulthood.

You've got to understand that life on the steppe wasn't easy. Families moved constantly, living off their livestock and dealing with brutal weather, raids from rival tribes, and whatever nature threw at them. There was no room for weakness. Wrestling was how boys learned to toughen up — physically and mentally. It wasn't just about throwing someone to the ground; it was about **building character**.

In those days, strength wasn't a luxury. It was a requirement. Wrestling taught boys that if you wanted respect, you had to earn it. Winning a match wasn't just a personal victory — it meant your community could count on you. It was proof that you were strong enough to protect your family and handle the tough life ahead.

A Boy's First Wrestling Match: A Defining Moment

When a boy wrestled in front of his community for the first time, it was a defining moment. His family, neighbors, and tribal leaders would gather to watch. This wasn't a casual match — it was a **test of readiness**. If the boy lost, it wasn't seen as a failure, but he was expected to learn from it. If he won, he earned respect, not just from his peers, but from the older men who'd been through it before him.

And this wasn't just about the fight itself. It was about how the boy **carried himself**. Was he respectful to his opponent? Did he follow the rules? Did he show determination and perseverance, even if he was on the verge of losing? All of these things mattered. The match was a way for the community to see if the boy had the right mindset to become a man.

Winning a match might earn you **gifts or titles**, but more importantly, it meant you were **trusted**. People would look at you and say, "This boy has potential. He can be relied on."

The Role of Wrestling in Shaping Masculinity

In Mongolian culture, wrestling wasn't just about being strong. It was about **embodying the ideal qualities of a man —** strength, patience, honor, and respect for tradition. A man who could wrestle well was seen as someone who could handle himself in tough situations. And believe me, in those days, life was nothing but tough situations.

There's an old saying in Mongolia: **"A man without wrestling is like a horse without a saddle."** It meant that strength and skill in wrestling defined what it meant to be a man. Wrestling wasn't something you did for fun. It was part of your identity.

And it wasn't just about brute strength. You had to be **clever and strategic**. Knowing when to push, when to pull, when to use your opponent's weight against them — it all required quick thinking. That's why smaller wrestlers could still win against bigger ones. It wasn't just muscle; it was about **skill and smarts**. And that's exactly what people respected.

Earning Honor Through Wrestling

In those days, honor was everything. Your reputation was your most valuable possession. Wrestling gave young men a chance to **earn their honor** in front of the entire community.

If you were a strong wrestler, people noticed. You weren't just seen as tough; you were seen as **reliable**. Someone people could trust in a fight or on a journey. Someone who wouldn't give up when things got hard.

And wrestling wasn't a one-time thing. You had to **prove yourself over and over**. Every match was a chance to build your reputation — or lose it. If you wrestled with honor, people respected you, even if you lost. But if you fought dirty or acted arrogantly, that reputation could be destroyed in an instant.

In fact, wrestlers were often used to **settle disputes** between tribes. Instead of going to war, leaders would hold wrestling matches. The outcome could determine peace or conflict. So, being a skilled wrestler didn't just benefit you personally — it could impact your whole community.

The Eagle Dance: More Than a Performance

Before a wrestling match, wrestlers would perform the **eagle dance**. This wasn't just for show. It was a way to **honor the sky god** and remind everyone that wrestling was more than a physical contest — it had a spiritual element too.

The dance symbolized **freedom, strength, and pride,** all qualities a man was expected to have. The wrestler would stretch his arms out like wings and move gracefully, mimicking an eagle in flight. This wasn't a random tradition — it was a way to connect wrestling to the spiritual beliefs of the Mongols. The eagle represented **power and resilience**, qualities every man wanted to embody.

The eagle dance was also a way to **calm the mind before a match.** It reminded wrestlers to stay focused, respect their opponents, and fight with honor. It wasn't about beating someone up. It was about testing yourself and proving your worth.

Winning Isn't Everything — But It Sure Helps

Now, let's be real. Winning mattered. If you were known as a great wrestler, it opened doors. You could **gain status**, **win prizes**, and even **attract better marriage prospects**. But it wasn't just about winning. It was about **how you won**.

A wrestler who fought with dignity and respect earned more admiration than someone who used dirty tactics to win. People valued **honor over victory**. If you showed good sportsmanship, people remembered that. If you disrespected your opponent, they remembered that too — for all the wrong reasons.

That's why wrestling was seen as a way to build **character**. It wasn't enough to be strong; you had to be honorable. That's the kind of man people trusted. That's the kind of man who could lead a family or even a tribe.

A Tradition That Lives On

The tradition of wrestling as a rite of passage is still alive today in Mongolia. Boys are still taught to wrestle from a young age, and the values it instills — **strength, respect, and perseverance** — remain important.

Even in modern times, wrestling is one of the most **respected professions** in Mongolia. The best wrestlers are given titles like **"Champion"** or **"Giant"**, and they're seen as national heroes. But at its core, the tradition hasn't changed. It's still about proving yourself, earning respect, and showing that you're capable of handling the challenges life throws at you.

In Mongolian culture, wrestling has always been more than just a sport. It's a way to **become a man**. It's about **earning your place** in the world, **showing your strength**, and **living with honor**. And that's why it's stood the test of time.

The Naadam Festival, Bökh Competitions, and Mongolian Identity

Let's talk about how Bökh wrestling went from something done casually in the fields to becoming one of the most important symbols of Mongolian culture. It's not just a sport for them — it's **part of who they are**. And a big part of that formalization comes down to the **Naadam Festival**, an annual event that celebrates the traditions and values that have defined Mongolian life for centuries.

Wrestling in Everyday Life Before It Was Formalized

Before wrestling became the structured event you see at Naadam today, it was already a big part of Mongolian life. People didn't need a special occasion to wrestle. It was something they did in the **open plains**, during family gatherings, or after long days of herding animals. Fathers would teach their sons, and matches could break out spontaneously as a way to settle disputes, pass the time, or test strength.

But even before it was formalized, wrestling wasn't just random grappling. It had **traditions, techniques, and even rituals** tied to the nomadic way of life. There were rules about respect, fairness, and conduct. It wasn't a street fight. It was about **honor, discipline, and balance**, values that mattered in both wrestling and everyday life.

The Naadam Festival: The Event That Formalized Bökh

Now, wrestling really became formalized through the **Naadam Festival**, which has been around for centuries. It's one of Mongolia's oldest and most important cultural events, and it's where **wrestling, horse racing, and archery** — the "Three Manly Skills" — come together.

Naadam started out as a **military celebration**. Genghis Khan and his generals would hold large gatherings to celebrate victories, honor warriors, and keep their soldiers fit. Wrestling competitions were part of these celebrations. Over time, what started as military games turned into an annual event for the entire community.

By the time the Mongol Empire expanded, Naadam was more than just a local festival. It became **a national tradition**, held every year to celebrate **strength, unity, and Mongolian identity**.

How Naadam Wrestling Works

The wrestling competitions at Naadam have their own **formal rules and structure**, which have remained pretty consistent for centuries. It's a single-elimination tournament — meaning, if you lose, you're out. But what's interesting is that **there are no weight classes**. That's right, a smaller wrestler can go up against a much bigger one, and it all comes down to **skill, balance, and strategy**.

The number of participants can vary, but the biggest Naadam festivals can have **512 wrestlers** competing in a single tournament. Matches are fought until one wrestler **touches the ground with any part of their body other than their**

feet. The winner remains standing, and the loser goes down. Simple rules, but tough to master.

And let me tell you, winning at Naadam **isn't just about bragging rights**. It's a huge honor. Winners are given **titles based on how many rounds they win**. Titles like **"Falcon," "Elephant," "Lion,"** and the highest one, **"Titan"** — these are badges of honor that stay with a wrestler for life.

Rituals and Traditions at Naadam

The wrestling at Naadam is **steeped in tradition**. It starts with the wrestlers doing the **eagle dance** before the match. This is more than just a warm-up. It's a **ritual to honor the spirits and the sky god Tengri**, showing respect to the sacred land and traditions.

The wrestlers wear a specific outfit — a **zodog** (a sleeveless jacket) and **shuudag** (shorts). There's a story behind the outfit. They say it was changed after a woman disguised herself as a man and won a wrestling tournament. To prevent that from happening again, the chest was left bare to show that only men were competing. Whether that story is true or not, the outfit has become a **symbol of tradition**.

Even the referees, known as **zasuul**, have a ceremonial role. They help guide the wrestlers, announce the results, and ensure the match follows traditional rules. The whole process is about more than competition — it's about **preserving cultural values**.

Bökh's Role in Mongolian Identity and Pride

For Mongolians, Bökh wrestling isn't just something they do at Naadam. It's a **core part of their national identity**. Wrestling is deeply tied to their **history as warriors and conquerors**. The idea that a person can rise through skill, strength, and discipline is a reflection of Mongolian culture as a whole.

Think about it — Genghis Khan himself was a wrestler. He used his strength and strategy, both on the wrestling field and the battlefield, to unite the Mongol tribes and build one of the largest empires in history. Mongolians see wrestling as a

connection to that legacy. It's a way of honoring their ancestors, their land, and their traditions.

Even today, Mongolia takes great pride in its wrestlers. The best wrestlers are **national heroes**, celebrated not just for their athletic ability but for what they represent: **resilience, strength, and loyalty to tradition**. In modern Mongolia, wrestling remains a symbol of **patriotism and cultural pride**.

Why Bökh Still Matters Today

Despite modern changes in society, wrestling still holds a **special place** in Mongolian culture. Every year, Naadam brings people together, both in Mongolia and among Mongolian communities around the world. It's a reminder of their **shared history and values**.

Wrestling teaches lessons that go beyond the ring:

- **Discipline**
- **Respect for tradition**
- **Strength in body and mind**

It's about **more than winning matches**. It's about carrying on the legacy of their ancestors, staying true to their roots, and showing pride in their culture. That's why Bökh isn't just a sport — it's a **symbol of who the Mongolian people are**.

So when you see those wrestlers at Naadam, it's not just about strength. It's about **honor, tradition, and identity**. It's about keeping alive a tradition that's lasted for centuries and will continue for many more.

The influence of Bökh on Mongolian identity and pride.

Bökh, the traditional wrestling of Mongolia, is deeply tied to the country's cultural identity and national pride. It is more than a sport. It functions as a social and historical institution that reflects the values of strength, endurance, and connection to the land. For centuries, it has been a way for Mongolians to demonstrate power, settle disputes, and uphold their customs. The practice of bökh shows how a physical tradition can shape a nation's identity, linking past generations to the present and reinforcing a shared sense of pride.

Wrestling has always been tied to survival in Mongolia. Life on the steppe was harsh, requiring physical strength and resilience to endure the environment. Bökh developed out of this reality. It wasn't performed in arenas or for leisure but as part of military training and preparation for life's challenges. During the era of Genghis Khan and his empire, wrestling was used to select the strongest warriors. The best wrestlers were celebrated not as entertainers but as critical figures in their communities—people who could be trusted to defend their families and tribes.

This connection between bökh and war made it an important symbol of Mongolian masculinity and leadership. A man's ability to wrestle well was seen as proof of his competence in battle and his capacity to take on responsibilities within his society. For centuries, every young boy learned to wrestle, and victories in wrestling matches were viewed as significant achievements that elevated a person's social status. Bökh wasn't separated from everyday life—it was a reflection of it.

The significance of bökh didn't fade with time. Even as Mongolia moved through various political systems, from the Mongol Empire to Qing rule, and later Soviet influence, bökh remained a core cultural practice. During periods of foreign domination, when Mongolian autonomy was limited, wrestling was one of the few traditions that continued to express Mongolian identity. The sight of men performing the eagle dance before a match and engaging in the same holds and throws their ancestors used centuries before created a sense of continuity. It reminded Mongolians that their culture and traditions persisted despite outside forces.

Wrestling titles also carry weight in shaping Mongolian identity. Winning a bökh tournament, especially at the Naadam Festival, isn't just a personal accomplishment. It's a public statement about who that person is within Mongolian society. Titles like *Zaan* (Elephant) and *Arslan* (Lion) carry cultural significance, symbolizing strength, resilience, and leadership. These titles are lifelong markers of status, and the wrestlers who earn them become national figures. For the broader population, these champions embody qualities that Mongolians value—tenacity, loyalty, and a deep connection to tradition.

The influence of bökh on Mongolian identity can also be seen in its rituals. The *zodog* and *shuudag*, the traditional wrestling attire, have remained largely unchanged for centuries. The open-chested design ensures transparency in the matches, but it also connects wrestlers to their predecessors. The eagle dance, performed before and after bouts, is a gesture of respect toward the land and sky, reinforcing Mongolia's spiritual connection to nature. These rituals are not just formalities—they are cultural markers that carry historical weight.

In rural areas, bökh remains a community event. Local competitions take place throughout the year, often during important gatherings. These matches aren't just about entertainment; they're social and cultural events where people come together to witness a living tradition. In many ways, the wrestlers on the field are seen as representatives of their local communities, carrying the pride of their families and regions with them. Victories bring respect not just to the wrestler but to the entire community he represents.

In modern Mongolia, bökh continues to play a role in shaping national pride. Even in a world increasingly influenced by globalization, the practice remains a distinctly Mongolian tradition. Schools and universities have wrestling programs, and major tournaments are broadcast nationwide. The annual Naadam Festival, where wrestling takes center stage, is a national holiday. The fact that wrestling remains one of the "Three Games of Men," alongside horse racing and archery, is a testament to how deeply embedded it is in the national consciousness.

Bökh also plays a role in preserving the Mongolian language and oral traditions. Wrestling matches are accompanied by traditional songs and the chanting of the wrestler's titles and victories. These verbal elements are important for keeping alive the unique sounds and phrases of the Mongolian language, particularly in rural areas where oral traditions still hold strong. Wrestlers are often praised in poetic verses, and these words become part of the local folklore, passed down through generations.

The influence of bökh on identity also ties into the Mongolian relationship with the land. Wrestling takes place outdoors, under open skies, reflecting the nomadic connection to nature. The ground on which a wrestler falls is seen as significant, symbolizing defeat or victory in the most primal sense. This bond with the land is a crucial part of the Mongolian worldview, and bökh reinforces it. Wrestling, for Mongolians, isn't confined to enclosed spaces—it happens where their ancestors roamed, in the natural world they have always revered.

In essence, bökh acts as a cultural anchor for Mongolia. It ties modern Mongolians to their history, reinforces social values, and provides a sense of pride in being part of a tradition that has endured for centuries. The wrestling champions of today are part of a continuous line that stretches back to the days of

Genghis Khan, carrying forward the legacy of a nation that values strength, resilience, and cultural heritage.

While other aspects of Mongolian life have changed with time, bökh remains a constant—a reminder of who the Mongolian people are and where they come from.

Chapter 4: Judo's Journey from Japan to Mongolia

The origins of Judo in Japan and its spread worldwide.

The origins of Judo take us back to the late 19th century, during a time of rapid modernization in Japan. The country was shedding centuries of feudal rule, opening itself to the wider world. But with this change came a question: how could Japan hold on to its identity, its traditions, while still modernizing? Enter **Kano Jigoro**, a man who would answer that question by taking something old—samurai-era jujutsu—and making it relevant to the new age.

Kano was born in 1860, during the dying days of the Tokugawa Shogunate, a time when samurai still walked the streets, but their swords were starting to lose relevance. He grew up witnessing the tension between tradition and progress. Jujutsu, the hand-to-hand combat method of the samurai, was fading into obscurity as Japan embraced firearms and Western-style military tactics. But Kano saw potential in the ancient art. He didn't just want to preserve it—he wanted to refine it, to strip away the deadly techniques and focus on something that would cultivate not only physical strength but also mental and moral development.

By 1882, Kano founded his own school, the **Kodokan**, in Tokyo. He called his new system **Judo**, meaning "the gentle way." But don't mistake "gentle" for weak. Judo is about balance, leverage, and using an opponent's strength against them. It teaches that victory doesn't come from brute force—it comes from strategy, adaptability, and timing. In a way, Judo itself became a metaphor for Japan's approach to modernization: adapt to the changes around you, use them to your advantage, and never forget your roots.

The philosophy behind Judo made it more than just a martial art. Kano wasn't interested in creating fighters. He was interested in creating well-rounded individuals. Judo was to be a way of life—a discipline that shaped character, fostered respect, and promoted continuous improvement. It became part of Japan's educational system and spread to police academies and military schools.

But here's where the story takes a turn. As Judo gained popularity in Japan, it didn't stay there. The world was watching, and soon, Judo began crossing borders.

By the early 20th century, Judo was introduced to Europe, the United States, and beyond. It became the first Asian martial art to gain global recognition. Kano himself traveled extensively to promote his art, and he played a significant role in getting Judo recognized as an Olympic sport. But its journey to Mongolia—**that** was something different.

When Judo arrived in Mongolia in the mid-20th century, it met a land with its own combat tradition: bökh. Mongolia didn't need an imported martial art to teach them about strength or discipline. Wrestling was already embedded in their culture. So why did Judo take root in Mongolia?

Because the two traditions, while different, shared common ground. Both emphasized respect, honor, and technique over sheer force. Both required patience, endurance, and mental fortitude. And both were more than sports—they were cultural institutions.

Mongolia first encountered Judo through Soviet influence. The Soviet Union had embraced Judo as part of its athletic programs, and since Mongolia was heavily aligned with the USSR at the time, the art made its way across the border. But unlike some foreign influences that are rejected as impositions, Judo resonated with the Mongolian people. They recognized something familiar in its principles—something that echoed their own values.

In the 1960s and 70s, Judo began to take hold in Mongolia, particularly among the urban youth. It offered a structured, formalized approach to grappling that complemented traditional wrestling. Mongolian wrestlers, already skilled in the art of throws and holds, found that they could transition into Judo with relative ease. And for a country that prided itself on its wrestling champions, Judo offered a new arena in which to prove their prowess on the international stage.

But it wasn't just about sport. For Mongolia, mastering Judo became a matter of national pride. Competing in Judo tournaments allowed Mongolians to step onto the world stage and showcase their strength and skill. And when Mongolian judokas began winning medals in international competitions, it wasn't just a victory for the athletes—it was a victory for the nation. It was proof that a small, landlocked country with a rich history of warriors could still stand tall in the modern world.

One of the most significant moments in this journey came at the **2008 Beijing Olympics**, when Mongolian judoka **Naidangiin Tüvshinbayar** won the country's first-ever Olympic gold medal. His victory wasn't just about personal achievement—it was a historic moment for Mongolia. It showed that the Mongolian fighting spirit, shaped by centuries of wrestling tradition, had found a new expression in Judo.

What's interesting is how Mongolia has made Judo its own. While the techniques and rules remain rooted in Kano's teachings, the Mongolian approach to Judo is distinct. It's aggressive, bold, and heavily influenced by bökh. Mongolian judokas often bring an intensity to the mat that reflects their wrestling heritage. Their grip-fighting style, their relentless pursuit of the throw—these are traits that set them apart from their competitors.

So, what started as a Japanese invention has become something more. In Mongolia, Judo isn't seen as a foreign import. It's become part of the fabric of Mongolian sports culture, standing alongside bökh and horse racing as a source of national pride. It's a reminder that traditions evolve, that cultures borrow from one another, and that identity is never fixed—it's always in motion.

The journey of Judo from Japan to Mongolia tells us something important. It shows that martial arts are never just about fighting. They carry philosophies, histories, and values with them. And when they move from one culture to another, they adapt, change, and take on new meanings. Judo, in Mongolia, has become more than just "the gentle way." It's a symbol of resilience, of adaptation, and of a proud nation continuing to make its mark on the world.

How Judo was introduced to Mongolia in the mid-20th century.

The introduction of Judo to Mongolia in the mid-20th century wasn't a smooth, organic evolution. It was shaped by geopolitics, cultural exchanges, and a deep, unshakable Mongolian connection to wrestling. It's a story tied to Mongolia's alignment with the Soviet Union, a partnership that profoundly influenced the country's education, military, and sports.

Let's set the stage. After the fall of the Qing dynasty in 1911, Mongolia declared independence, but it wasn't long before its fate became entangled in the growing power struggles between Russia and China. By the 1920s, Mongolia became a satellite state of the Soviet Union, adopting socialist policies and aligning itself with Soviet ideology. This partnership wasn't just about politics—it touched every aspect of Mongolian life, including sports.

In the Soviet Union, Judo was already being embraced as a practical combat sport. The Soviets admired its structured discipline and found it adaptable to military training. But the

Soviets didn't adopt traditional Japanese Judo without modification. They developed **Sambo**, a hybrid martial art that blended Judo techniques with elements of traditional Russian wrestling. Soviet athletes trained rigorously in both Sambo and Judo, and these combat sports became central to Soviet physical education programs. It was only a matter of time before these practices made their way to Mongolia.

In the late 1940s and early 1950s, Mongolian students, athletes, and military officers began traveling to the Soviet Union for education and training. This was part of a broader Soviet initiative to strengthen ties with its allies by offering them access to its universities and military academies. Among the subjects taught in these institutions were martial arts, including both Sambo and Judo.

The first Mongolian athletes exposed to Judo encountered it through these Soviet training programs. Initially, Judo wasn't seen as a sport for the general population. It was primarily taught to military officers and law enforcement personnel, who appreciated its practical applications for self-defense and control techniques. But as these officers returned home, they brought the art with them, planting the seeds for Judo's growth in Mongolia.

One of the key moments in Judo's introduction to Mongolia came in the early 1960s. During this period, the Mongolian government, heavily influenced by Soviet policies, began formalizing its national sports programs. Wrestling, of course, was already deeply entrenched in Mongolian culture, but there was a growing recognition that participating in international sports competitions could be a way for Mongolia to assert itself on the world stage. Judo, with its inclusion in global competitions like the Olympics, became an attractive option.

In 1964, Judo made its debut as an Olympic sport at the **Tokyo Games**. The timing was significant. For Mongolia, which had gained recognition as a sovereign state in 1961 when it joined the United Nations, the 1960s were a period of growing national identity and international ambition. The Mongolian government saw sports as a way to strengthen national pride and gain international recognition. Judo, as a structured, codified martial art with global prestige, fit perfectly into this vision.

Mongolian athletes began receiving formal Judo training in Soviet sports academies, and by the late 1960s, Mongolia established its own Judo federation. Initially, there was skepticism. Wrestling, or bökh, was still king. Why should Mongolians, who had been wrestling for centuries, adopt a foreign martial art?

The answer was competition. Wrestling was a national tradition, but it wasn't an Olympic sport. Judo, on the other hand, offered a path to international recognition. For a small, landlocked country that had long existed in the shadow of larger powers, the prospect of earning medals on the world stage was irresistible.

The first Mongolian Judo competitions were modest, often held alongside traditional wrestling events. But it quickly became apparent that Mongolian wrestlers had a natural affinity for Judo. Their experience in bökh gave them an edge. They already knew how to grapple, how to throw opponents, how to use leverage to their advantage. All they needed was to learn the rules and strategies specific to Judo.

By the 1970s, Mongolian Judo was growing rapidly. The national team began competing in international tournaments, and Mongolian judokas gained a reputation for their aggressive, relentless style—a style clearly influenced by bökh.

While other countries approached Judo with careful precision, the Mongolians brought the raw energy of the steppe to the mat. Their throws were powerful, their grip-fighting fierce, and their endurance unmatched.

One of the pivotal figures in this early period was **Tsendiin Damdin**, a former wrestler who became one of Mongolia's first Judo champions. Damdin's success showed that Mongolian athletes could excel in Judo on the world stage. His victories weren't just personal triumphs—they were a validation of the government's decision to embrace Judo as part of Mongolia's national sports program.

By the 1980s, Judo was firmly established in Mongolia. Training centers sprang up across the country, and Judo became a popular sport among young athletes. What had started as a military training tool had transformed into a national passion. Today, Judo is as much a part of Mongolian sports culture as bökh. And while it may have come from Japan, it has taken on a distinctly Mongolian character.

The journey of Judo to Mongolia wasn't a simple transfer of knowledge from one country to another. It was shaped by historical forces—by geopolitics, cultural exchange, and national ambition. It arrived during a period when Mongolia was redefining itself on the global stage, and it became a way for the country to assert its strength, its resilience, and its identity.

Judo in Mongolia is more than an imported martial art. It's a story of adaptation, of blending tradition with modernity, and of a nation finding new ways to express its ancient values. What began as a Japanese discipline now carries the spirit of the Mongolian steppe, where strength and honor have always been paramount.

Chapter 5: The Soviet Era and Judo's Institutionalization

The role of Soviet influence in promoting Judo in Mongolia.

The Soviet era swept across Mongolia like a cold, relentless wind, reshaping every corner of life. In the first half of the 20th century, Mongolia stood as a nation caught between tradition and the weight of foreign powers, with its own identity at risk of being overshadowed. Yet amid this upheaval, a new force quietly entered the Mongolian spirit—a force that would forever intertwine Mongolia's destiny with a martial art from distant Japan. That art was judo.

Mongolia had long been a land of fierce warriors. Wrestling, or **bökh**, had been part of Mongolian culture for centuries, celebrated in festivals and ceremonies that paid homage to strength, endurance, and the primal art of combat. But by the mid-20th century, wrestling alone was not enough. A changing world demanded new skills, new disciplines, and new alliances. As Mongolia fell deeper into the Soviet sphere of influence, the Soviets brought not just political ideologies but also a fascination with martial arts that could be channeled toward their vision of disciplined, modern athletes. It was through this lens that judo came to be seen as more than just a sport. It was a tool of unity, a way to shape the ideal citizen—strong, disciplined, loyal, and resilient.

The Soviet Union, always eager to exert its influence, saw an opportunity in the sport of judo. By the 1940s, judo had already made its way into the Soviet athletic system, which prized combat sports as a way to build both physical prowess and ideological loyalty. For the Soviets, martial arts were never just about physical competition. They were a means of cultivating the "New Soviet Man"—someone who embodied strength, discipline, and loyalty to the state. Judo, with its focus on respect, control, and mental fortitude, fit neatly into this philosophy.

In Mongolia, the arrival of judo was both timely and transformative. The nation, still recovering from its nomadic past and adjusting to the influence of communism, found in judo a curious blend of tradition and modernity. Though judo was Japanese in origin, it shared deep similarities with Mongolia's own wrestling traditions. Both arts emphasized balance, leverage, and the ability to overpower one's opponent without brute strength. Judo's philosophy of "maximum efficiency with minimum effort" resonated with Mongolian warriors who understood that skill often triumphed over sheer size.

The Soviets wasted no time embedding judo into Mongolia's growing athletic programs. In the 1950s, Soviet coaches and trainers began arriving in Ulaanbaatar, bringing with them not just techniques but a system—a framework for turning judo into an institutionalized sport. They taught Mongolian athletes how to compete on the world stage, emphasizing discipline and mental resilience alongside physical training. Soviet influence was pervasive, shaping the very way Mongolian judo practitioners thought about the sport. It was no longer just a martial art; it was a symbol of national pride, a way to prove Mongolia's strength on the international stage.

But the rise of judo in Mongolia was not without tension. For a nation that had spent centuries resisting outside forces, there was an inherent irony in embracing a martial art with foreign roots. Yet Mongolians did what they had always done—they made it their own. Judo in Mongolia became more than just a

Soviet import. It blended with local traditions, drawing on the spirit of **bökh** while adopting the formal structure of judo's Japanese origins. The result was a unique style, one that would eventually take the judo world by storm.

Mongolian athletes, shaped by the harsh landscape and centuries of wrestling tradition, took naturally to the sport. They were agile, strong, and unyielding—traits that translated perfectly into judo's demanding techniques. By the 1960s, Mongolia was producing judo athletes who could hold their own against the world's best. The country's first international judo appearances were modest, but each victory carried symbolic weight. These athletes were not just competitors; they were ambassadors of a nation that refused to be overshadowed by larger powers.

As the Soviet-Mongolian relationship deepened, so too did the institutionalization of judo. The Mongolian government, encouraged by Soviet advisors, invested heavily in athletic programs, seeing judo as a way to forge national unity and bolster international prestige. Training centers sprang up across the country. Promising young wrestlers were recruited and taught the ways of judo. Competitions became grand events, drawing crowds eager to witness their nation's strength on display.

For Mongolian athletes, judo was both a challenge and an opportunity. It required them to learn new techniques, to adapt to a sport that demanded precision and strategy. But it also offered something invaluable—a path to international recognition. In a world dominated by Cold War politics, sporting success became a way for smaller nations to assert themselves. Every match won by a Mongolian judoka was a statement: Mongolia was here, strong and proud.

Yet judo in Mongolia never lost its connection to the past. Even as athletes donned their gi and bowed before entering the mat, they carried with them the spirit of their ancestors—the wrestlers who had grappled on the steppes, the warriors who had ridden into battle under Genghis Khan's banner. Judo, though foreign in origin, became a new way to honor an old tradition. It was a bridge between past and present, between Mongolia's nomadic heritage and its modern aspirations.

By the time Mongolia earned its first significant victories in judo, the sport had become deeply woven into the nation's fabric. It was no longer just a Soviet import; it was a Mongolian art form, shaped by the unique spirit of a people who refused to be conquered. The Soviets may have brought judo to Mongolia, but it was the Mongolians who breathed life into it, making it their own.

In the decades that followed, Mongolian judokas would go on to achieve great success on the world stage. They would stand atop podiums, their nation's flag rising behind them, proving that a small nation with a big heart could compete with the best. But behind every victory was the story of a journey—one that began in the Soviet era, when a foreign martial art found a new home in the land of the eternal blue sky.=

The fusion of Bökh techniques with Judo philosophy.

Mongolia's soul has always been tied to wrestling. **Bökh,** the traditional wrestling style of the steppe, is more than a sport—it is a cultural cornerstone, a test of strength, will, and honor. It is said that no true Mongolian celebration is complete without a wrestling match. For centuries, **bökh** champions were revered not just as athletes but as symbols of the nation's enduring spirit. Their strength was the strength of Mongolia itself, unshakable as the mountains, resilient as the endless grasslands.

When judo arrived, it did not displace **bökh**. Instead, the two forms of wrestling—one ancient and homegrown, the other modern and imported—began to merge in ways that would redefine both. Judo's philosophy of technique over brute strength found fertile ground in a culture that had always valued cunning as much as power. Mongolian wrestlers, who had grown up mastering **bökh's** throws and grapples, saw in judo a new canvas on which to paint their skills.

But this fusion was not just about technique; it was also about mindset. Judo, with its guiding principle of **"Seiryoku Zenyo"**—maximum efficiency with minimum effort—aligned naturally with the way Mongolian wrestlers approached combat. The vast Mongolian landscape, harsh and unforgiving, had taught its people that survival depended not on overwhelming force, but on adaptability and endurance. The steppes demanded cleverness, agility, and an unyielding spirit—all traits that **bökh** wrestlers embodied. These qualities now found a new expression on the judo mat.

One of the most striking contributions that **bökh** made to Mongolian judo was its unique array of throws. In **bökh**, wrestlers often rely on powerful hip throws and leg sweeps, techniques designed to bring opponents crashing to the ground with force. These moves translated seamlessly into judo, where the aim is to unbalance one's opponent and execute a decisive throw. Mongolian judokas began to incorporate these traditional wrestling moves into their judo repertoire, surprising their opponents with techniques unfamiliar to the broader judo world.

The **tsuurankhai**, a signature throw in **bökh**, became a favorite of Mongolian judokas. This throw, which uses the hips and upper body to flip an opponent over, mirrors judo's **harai goshi** and **uchi mata** techniques but with a distinct Mongolian flavor. Mongolian athletes also brought the **shuudarga** grip—a deep, firm hold around the opponent's waist—to the judo mat, adding an aggressive, unrelenting style to their matches. Even the way Mongolian wrestlers controlled their balance and leveraged their body weight became an advantage in judo competitions.

Yet, it wasn't only the techniques that made this fusion unique. The spiritual connection between **bökh** and judo ran deep. In both arts, respect for one's opponent and humility in victory were paramount. Judo's emphasis on discipline, honor, and mutual benefit resonated with Mongolian wrestlers, who had always believed that the true measure of a man was not just in his victories, but in his conduct. This shared philosophy made the transition from **bökh** to judo feel less like adopting a foreign sport and more like rediscovering something that had always been there.

For the Soviets, who viewed judo as a tool for building disciplined citizens, this fusion was unexpected. They had assumed Mongolia would simply follow the Soviet model, adopting the techniques and philosophies passed down from Moscow. But Mongolian judokas defied expectations, bringing their unique wrestling traditions to the mat and reshaping the sport itself. What emerged was a distinct style—ferocious yet technical, aggressive yet controlled. It was a style born of the steppe, forged by centuries of wrestling tradition, but refined through judo's structured discipline.

This blend of **bökh** and judo also transformed Mongolia's wrestling culture. Young boys who once dreamed only of becoming **bökh** champions now saw a new path before them—a path that could take them beyond Mongolia's borders, to the great arenas of the world. Judo offered something **bökh** could not: international recognition, a chance to prove Mongolian strength on a global stage.

But even as Mongolian judokas traveled the world, winning medals and making headlines, they never forgot their roots. In every match, the spirit of **bökh** could be seen in their movements—the way they held their opponents, the precision of their throws, the unshakeable determination in their eyes. It was as if the ancient warriors of Mongolia had stepped onto the mat, carrying with them the legacy of a thousand wrestling matches under the open sky.

The fusion of **bökh** and judo created something unique: a fighting style that was both ancient and modern, both local and global. It was a reminder that traditions do not die; they evolve, adapt, and endure. Mongolian judokas carried their heritage into every match, proving that a nation's identity can be preserved even as it transforms.

In the decades to come, this fusion would become Mongolia's signature in the world of judo. Their wrestlers would be known for their relentless, attacking style—a style that blended the raw strength of the steppe with the refined techniques of the dojo. And while the world might see them as judo champions, in their hearts, they would always remain **bökh** wrestlers—warriors of the eternal blue sky.

Establishment of Judo clubs, competitions, and formal training.

In the early days of the Soviet Union, after the 1917 Revolution, there was a strong desire to build a new society, one that was healthier, stronger, and more disciplined. Martial arts were seen as a way to achieve this, and judo, which had gained some popularity in Japan and elsewhere, became one of the martial arts the Soviet leadership began to take an interest in. But like many things in the early Soviet years, the path wasn't straightforward. The establishment of judo clubs, the first competitions, and formal training systems had to work within a context of political upheaval, ideological conflicts, and the gradual shaping of Soviet sporting identity.

Judo's introduction to the Soviet Union can be traced back to the 1920s, when the Soviet state began to look at various sports from around the world to foster physical strength and discipline. The early years were filled with trials and experiments. Judo, then known as "Japanese wrestling" in many circles, was first introduced by individuals who were keen to bring this discipline to the masses. One of the early figures in this movement was a man named Vladimir Korkin. Korkin, a keen sportsman himself, had studied judo abroad in Japan and brought back knowledge and techniques that would shape the first judo training in the USSR. But this was no simple task.

The 1920s and 1930s in the Soviet Union were a time of intense political change. There was a push for all sports to be aligned with the communist ideology, and that meant certain practices were either embraced or rejected based on their perceived usefulness to the state. Judo, with its emphasis on discipline, respect, and physical endurance, appealed to the authorities. It had a structured system of ranks, clear rules of combat, and, most importantly, a strong educational component that resonated with the Soviet desire to develop "new men and women" for the socialist state. However, for a while, judo was met with suspicion, primarily because of its Japanese origins, and its perceived foreignness made some Soviet officials hesitant to fully embrace it.

Over time, though, the arguments in favor of judo began to outweigh the political hesitations. It was especially attractive because it focused on leverage, technique, and grappling rather than brute strength. This made it accessible to a broader range of people, including those who might not have been built for traditional sports like weightlifting or running. In the late 1930s, the first Soviet judo clubs began to emerge, particularly in cities like Moscow and Leningrad (now St. Petersburg). These clubs were small at first, with a few passionate individuals training under the guidance of instructors who had either studied judo abroad or were self-taught.

Formal competitions began to emerge in the 1940s, and it was then that judo really started to take off. By this time, there was a growing push from the Soviet leadership to build a sporting system that would compete on the world stage. The state was not only interested in fitness for personal development but also in demonstrating Soviet superiority in all areas, including sports. Judo competitions in the USSR were organized as part of this vision. While early tournaments were modest affairs, they gradually grew in scale, with regional and national events drawing more competitors from all over the country.

In the post-war years, as the Soviet state solidified its grip on power, sports became a tool for international prestige. The authorities realized that sporting victories could show the world the strength of the Soviet system. By the 1950s and 1960s, judo had solidified itself as a respected sport in the Soviet Union. This was helped by the rise of a formal training structure, which the government set up to ensure the athletes were both physically and mentally prepared for competition.

The judo system in the Soviet Union was unique, as it was highly regimented. Athletes were trained not only in the techniques and movements of judo but also in the philosophy of the sport. The Soviet authorities used judo to instill values such as perseverance, discipline, and respect for authority, all of which were important in the broader context of the Soviet state. There was a clear emphasis on collective over individual achievements, and the development of the sport was tied to the larger project of Soviet identity and pride. Training camps were often held in isolated areas, away from the distractions of everyday life, where athletes could focus entirely on perfecting their skills.

The formalization of judo in the Soviet Union also led to the development of a strong competitive structure. The Soviet Union became one of the dominant forces in international judo by the 1960s, producing world-class athletes who competed successfully at global competitions. Athletes like Vasili Shidlovskiy and Boris Gurevich became well-known figures in the judo world, and their successes helped to raise the profile of the sport within the USSR. The Soviet judo system was based on a rigid, state-controlled model, and competitors often followed a set path that included years of rigorous training, national tournaments, and, for the best, opportunities to compete at the highest international levels.

By the time the 1970s arrived, judo had become firmly embedded in the Soviet sporting culture. Training centers were now established across the Union, and judo was seen as a key part of Soviet sports culture. This was reflected in the rise of sports academies where future champions were identified and molded. These academies took athletes from a young age and placed them in highly structured environments designed to push their physical and mental limits.

Even as judo became more formalized, the spirit of camaraderie and discipline that characterized the sport continued to influence those who practiced it. Judo clubs often became tight-knit communities where members shared not only a passion for the sport but also a deep sense of loyalty to one another. These clubs were places where young people, especially in the post-war years, found not only physical strength but also a sense of belonging and purpose. For many, the journey through the judo system was about more than just winning medals; it was about building character, discipline, and unity, all of which were central to the Soviet vision of what it meant to be a citizen of the Union.

As the years passed and the Soviet Union eventually collapsed, judo remained a staple of Russian sporting life. The clubs and training systems that had been established during those early years in the Soviet era had lasting effects, influencing future generations of athletes. Though the political landscape had changed, the discipline and structure that had been developed over decades remained. The legacy of the Soviet era's approach to judo can still be seen in modern Russian judo, which continues to be one of the strongest in the world today.

Chapter 6: Adapting Traditional Wrestling to Judo Techniques

How Mongolian wrestlers adapted their Bökh skills to excel in Judo.

In the heart of the Soviet Union, during the mid-20th century, a unique blend of cultural influences began to shape the world of competitive sports, especially judo. One of the most remarkable adaptations occurred in the Soviet republic of Mongolia, where wrestlers with a deep-rooted tradition in Bökh, the ancient Mongolian style of wrestling, began to adapt their skills to the rapidly growing world of judo. The Mongolian wrestlers didn't just add judo techniques to their existing training—they transformed their traditional wrestling knowledge into a powerful new style that helped them excel in the international judo scene.

Mongolian wrestling, or Bökh, had been practiced for centuries. It was an integral part of Mongolian culture, deeply embedded in their history, folklore, and daily life. Unlike many other forms of wrestling, Bökh was known for its emphasis on agility, balance, and leverage rather than sheer strength. Wrestlers were trained to use their opponent's movements against them, a principle that mirrored many of the techniques found in judo. Bökh wrestlers relied heavily on throws, grips, and body manipulation, which made the transition to judo somewhat natural for them.

When Mongolia became part of the Soviet sphere in the 1920s and 1930s, and judo started to gain traction within the Soviet sporting system, many Mongolian athletes saw the potential of the sport. They were drawn to judo's strategic focus on throws, pins, and submissions, which closely resembled the techniques they had mastered in their own wrestling culture. However, while judo's official techniques were highly structured and codified, Bökh had a more fluid, less formalized approach to combat, relying on an intuitive understanding of balance, timing, and leverage.

Initially, many Mongolian wrestlers were skeptical about adopting the rigid rules of judo. Judo had strict regulations on grips, stances, and movements, and the emphasis on the "tatami" (the mat) was different from the open-air, free-flowing style of Bökh. But over time, these wrestlers began to see how they could adapt their techniques to fit the judo framework without losing their traditional edge.

One of the first changes came in the area of grips. In Bökh, the wrestlers often used a wide variety of holds and grips, depending on the situation. Some of these were very different from judo's more controlled methods. Mongolian wrestlers were adept at finding an opponent's weak points, and they often relied on quick, powerful pulls and twists. When they started to train in judo, they adapted their natural gripping instincts to the more structured rules of judo. The Mongolian approach to gripping was often aggressive and unorthodox, which caught many judo opponents off guard. They learned how to control their opponents' balance early in the match, disrupting their opponent's flow and setting them up for throws, just like in Bökh.

Another area where Mongolian wrestlers excelled was in the use of body position and leverage. Bökh places great importance on being able to control your opponent's center of gravity, and this transferred directly to judo's throws. A judo throw, like the famous *ippon seoi nage* or *osoto gari*, requires perfect timing and an ability to use your opponent's momentum against them. Mongolian wrestlers, with their finely tuned sense of balance, could often execute these throws with remarkable precision. They didn't just learn the textbook versions of the judo throws; they added their own flair, using angles and grips that were more characteristic of Bökh, where there was often a greater focus on angles of attack rather than sheer force.

The Mongolian wrestlers' adaptability was also reflected in their mental approach to the sport. Bökh had always emphasized mental toughness and perseverance. In their tradition, a match wasn't just about physical dominance; it was about outwitting your opponent, staying calm under pressure, and waiting for the right moment to strike. These traits made Mongolian judo practitioners incredibly resilient. They could often outlast their opponents in matches, staying focused on the bigger picture of winning rather than just individual techniques. This was a crucial skill in judo, where patience and strategy often led to victory, especially in longer, more grueling matches.

As the Soviet Union embraced judo more fully, with its emphasis on competing on the global stage, Mongolian judo began to evolve. The Soviet training camps, which were often rigorous and highly disciplined, helped refine the Mongolian approach. Soviet trainers, who had their own deep understanding of judo techniques, quickly realized the potential in the Mongolian wrestlers. They didn't try to strip away the traditional elements of Bökh; instead, they allowed the wrestlers to incorporate these into their judo training. This approach proved incredibly effective.

In the 1960s and 1970s, Mongolian athletes began to emerge as world-class competitors in judo. They took what they had learned from their traditional wrestling roots and combined it with the structured methods of judo, creating a unique style that made them stand out on the world stage. At international competitions, Mongolian judo practitioners were known for their aggressive and dynamic techniques, often surprising their opponents with their unconventional approaches. They were masters at controlling the center of the mat, dictating the pace of the match, and applying pressure from unexpected angles.

One of the most successful Mongolian judoka of this era was Tsagaanbaatar, who became famous for his ability to use traditional Bökh grips in judo tournaments. His performances at the World Judo Championships in the 1970s helped establish

Mongolia's reputation as a judo powerhouse within the Soviet Union. His success was a testament to how Mongolian wrestlers had taken the best elements of their wrestling heritage and adapted them to judo.

By the 1980s, the blend of Bökh and judo had become a hallmark of Mongolian judo, influencing generations of athletes. This fusion of styles allowed Mongolia to punch above its weight in international judo competitions, consistently sending athletes to the top of the podium in world tournaments. Mongolian judo's success wasn't just about the technical skills of the wrestlers; it was also about their unshakeable mental toughness and the rich cultural heritage that shaped them.

Ultimately, the ability of Mongolian wrestlers to adapt their Bökh skills to judo wasn't just a matter of incorporating new techniques—it was about maintaining their cultural identity while mastering a new form of combat. It was this balance between tradition and innovation that helped Mongolia carve out its place on the world judo stage, blending two worlds in a way that no other country had. Their success would inspire future generations to view judo not just as a sport, but as a dynamic fusion of cultures, where history and innovation could come together to create something truly powerful.

The unique Mongolian approach to Judo throws and grappling.

Key differences and similarities between Bökh and Judo.

Mongolian judo, shaped by its ancient roots in Bökh, has always been a fascinating blend of traditional wrestling and modern martial arts. The Mongolian approach to judo throws and grappling reflects this rich wrestling heritage, and it brings unique elements to the sport that set it apart from the standard judo techniques seen in other parts of the world. The interplay between these two styles—Bökh and judo—offers both striking similarities and distinct differences, and understanding these elements sheds light on why Mongolian judoka became such formidable competitors on the global stage.

Bökh, the traditional Mongolian wrestling style, has been practiced for centuries. It is deeply embedded in Mongolian culture, and its origins are tied to the nomadic lifestyle of the Mongol people. Bökh is known for its emphasis on balance, leverage, and quick, decisive moves, and much of its philosophy revolves around using the opponent's energy against them. This focus on balance and fluidity made Bökh particularly well-suited to complement the principles of judo, which also emphasizes throws, balance disruption, and using an opponent's movement to your advantage.

One of the fundamental aspects of Bökh wrestling is its fluid approach to throws. Unlike other traditional wrestling styles that focus on brute strength, Bökh emphasizes technique and timing, relying on the wrestler's ability to outmaneuver and outsmart their opponent rather than overpower them. This principle resonates with judo, which is built around the concept of *jū*, meaning "gentleness" or "flexibility." In both sports, the goal is to use leverage and timing to throw the opponent, making size and strength less important than agility, control, and precision.

Mongolian wrestlers, transitioning to judo, did not have to start from scratch. Their experience in Bökh gave them a natural affinity for some of the most important judo techniques, particularly the throws. Judo throws, like *ippon seoi nage* (shoulder throw) and *osoto gari* (major outer reaping throw), require a keen sense of balance and the ability to anticipate the opponent's movements. In Bökh, wrestlers often used similar techniques, though with a slightly different emphasis. In Bökh, throws were often set up quickly and decisively, and the use of quick grips and leverage played a central role. Mongolian wrestlers brought this same aggressiveness and fluidity to judo, adapting the traditional throws to the structured world of judo competition.

One of the most notable features of the Mongolian approach to judo is how they modify grips and body positioning. In judo, there are strict rules about how and where you can grip your opponent's gi (uniform). These rules are designed to prevent overly aggressive or unsafe techniques, ensuring that the competition remains fair and controlled. But Mongolian wrestlers, having spent years in Bökh, often found themselves adapting their wrestling instincts to fit the judo structure. In Bökh, wrestlers were taught to seize any opportunity to grip or manipulate their opponent's body to gain an advantage. This led to a more aggressive, sometimes unorthodox approach to judo grips. For example, while judo places more emphasis on controlling the opponent's sleeves or lapels, Mongolian judoka might use a wider variety of grips, including those that target the opponent's wrists, collar, or even the belt.

Additionally, the speed at which Mongolian wrestlers transitioned into judo throws set them apart from others. In Bökh, wrestlers were trained to attack quickly, often throwing their opponent within the first few seconds of contact. This rapid tempo was a key feature of Mongolian judo as well. While many judo practitioners spend considerable time maneuvering to establish the ideal grip and position, Mongolian judoka would often launch their attacks almost immediately, catching their opponents off guard. Their throws were often fast, aggressive, and sometimes less predictable. They capitalized on every opening, staying aggressive from the start to maintain control over the match.

However, despite these differences in approach, there are striking similarities between Bökh and judo. Both share an emphasis on balance, timing, and fluidity. In both disciplines, wrestlers or judoka are taught to understand the importance of using the opponent's momentum against them. For instance, in judo's *tai otoshi* (body drop), the key is to create a situation where your opponent's center of gravity is disrupted, allowing you to perform a quick and effective throw. In Bökh, similar techniques exist, where the wrestler manipulates the opponent's balance, using the opponent's own weight and momentum to execute a successful throw. Mongolian wrestlers transitioning into judo found that this shared principle of balance made it easier for them to adapt to the new sport.

Another similarity is the use of *maai*, the concept of distance and timing, which is crucial in both sports. In Bökh, wrestlers constantly assess the distance between themselves and their opponent, looking for opportunities to strike or throw when the moment is right. Similarly, judo places a high value on *maai*, as the judoka must understand when to attack, when to defend, and when to create space to set up a throw. Mongolian judo practitioners, accustomed to the quick footwork and precise timing required in Bökh, excelled in this aspect of the sport. Their ability to close the gap quickly, judge timing, and strike decisively was one of the key factors that made them successful in judo competitions.

However, despite these similarities, there are clear differences between the two sports as well. The most significant difference lies in the mat rules. In judo, the mat is a defined space, and the action is contained within its boundaries. A judoka must be aware of both their positioning and their opponent's movements within this confined space. Bökh, on the other hand, was traditionally practiced in an open field or on a dirt surface, with little to no boundaries. This meant that the strategy in Bökh could be more free-flowing, with wrestlers using the environment to their advantage. The confinement of the judo mat required Mongolian wrestlers to adapt their techniques slightly, focusing more on controlling the opponent's movements and timing within a set space.

Moreover, judo places a greater emphasis on *ne-waza*, or ground fighting, than Bökh, where throws are the primary focus. Judo has a complex system of pins, submissions, and transitions from standing to ground techniques. While Mongolian wrestlers were certainly skilled in controlling their opponents and could adapt to the ground game, the mental shift from focusing on throws to being proficient on the ground took time. This was one of the challenges Mongolian judoka faced as they adapted their wrestling background to judo's more comprehensive system.

In the end, the Mongolian approach to judo throws and grappling stands out for its aggressive, fluid, and instinctive nature. Mongolian judoka integrated their Bökh background with judo's rules and techniques, creating a unique style that set them apart from other competitors. The fusion of their traditional wrestling techniques with the discipline of judo not only made them formidable on the world stage but also proved that the adaptation of traditional skills to modern competition could create something truly powerful.

Chapter 7: The First Mongolian Judo Champions

The first time Mongolian judo stepped onto the international stage was a moment of both excitement and uncertainty. It was the 1960s, a time when Mongolia, nestled within the vast expanse of the Soviet Union, had already begun to make its mark in various sports. But judo, at that point, was still a young discipline in Mongolia. Although the Mongolian wrestlers had adapted their traditional Bökh techniques to the rigid structure of judo, the idea of competing on a global scale was still new and intimidating. It was a leap into the unknown, where the challenges were as much about overcoming skepticism within their own country as they were about facing opponents from more established judo nations.

In those early years, the Soviet Union had already developed a formidable reputation in judo. The Soviet judo players were disciplined, well-coached, and prepared for competition at the highest levels. Mongolia, with its unique blend of wrestling traditions and newly acquired judo techniques, was still a newcomer, and yet, they were determined. There was a rawness to their approach—no one expected them to take over the sport, but they were fueled by something more than just technique. The Mongolians had pride, passion, and a will to prove themselves. They were ready to show the world that they belonged in the competitive arena.

Mongolia's first foray into international judo competition came in the form of the 1965 World Judo Championships, held in Paris. At the time, judo was still developing as a global sport, but it was already growing fast in countries like Japan, France, and the Soviet Union. For Mongolia, sending athletes to compete in this prestigious tournament was an act of boldness. The athletes chosen for this mission were young, relatively untested, but they had something their opponents might not: a deep-rooted wrestling culture that, when fused with judo, gave them an unpredictable edge.

The Mongolian delegation was small, and their expectations were cautious. After all, these athletes had little experience in international competitions, and the world of judo was far different from the practice rooms in Ulaanbaatar or the open fields where they had trained in their traditional wrestling.

They were underprepared in many ways, lacking the depth of technique and strategy seen in their counterparts from countries with long-established judo traditions. But what they lacked in experience, they made up for with grit, determination, and a hunger to succeed.

On the mat, the Mongolian judoka made a strong, immediate impression. At first, the international community was unsure of what to make of them. Their style was aggressive, raw, and unpolished. They attacked with a fierceness that surprised their more seasoned opponents. Mongolian judo athletes were known for executing throws with a speed and decisiveness that few could anticipate. They were unpredictable, using their wrestling instincts to get inside their opponent's defenses, and once they had their grip, they struck swiftly.

But there were moments of doubt too. The Mongolian competitors often found themselves at a disadvantage when it came to stamina and familiarity with the intricate rules of judo competition. Unlike their opponents, who had spent years perfecting their grip techniques, throws, and ground fighting, the Mongolians were still getting accustomed to the finer points of the sport. They struggled with the transitions between standing techniques and ground fighting, where judo placed a significant emphasis.

Yet, despite these growing pains, Mongolia's first-ever appearance at an international judo event ended up being more than just a learning experience. It became a statement. The Mongolian athletes, despite being raw and inexperienced, were able to hold their own, and even more impressively, one of them made it to the podium. The victory was a shock to the judo world, but not to the Mongolian team. They had trained relentlessly, adapting their Bökh techniques and infusing them with the principles of judo. They didn't just want to compete; they wanted to win.

The athlete who made history was a young judoka named Tsagaanbaatar. His victory was unexpected, but it was also a product of the resilience that was a hallmark of Mongolian athletes. Tsagaanbaatar's skill on the mat was a blend of his Bökh foundation and his judo training. His ability to close the distance between him and his opponent with lightning speed, his precision in executing throws, and his ability to throw his opponents off-balance—these were traits that had been honed in Mongolia's wrestling fields. It wasn't the textbook style of judo, but it worked. His victory was proof that the Mongolian approach to judo—an approach that blended their centuries-old wrestling techniques with new judo strategies—was not just viable but effective on the international stage.

Tsagaanbaatar's win reverberated throughout the judo community. It was a triumph not just for Mongolia, but for a new way of approaching judo. For the first time, the world saw that judo could be shaped by other wrestling traditions and that countries with less experience in the sport could still challenge the established powers. Mongolia's success was a testament to the power of cultural adaptation, of combining ancient traditions with modern sports techniques, and of the tenacity that comes from years of wrestling under the open skies of Mongolia's steppes.

In the years that followed, Mongolia's involvement in international judo competitions continued to grow. The nation, encouraged by Tsagaanbaatar's success, poured more resources into judo training, refining their techniques, and sending more athletes to compete abroad. The next generation of Mongolian judo athletes followed in Tsagaanbaatar's footsteps, carrying the legacy of their traditional wrestling while refining their judo skills to become even more formidable competitors.

Mongolia's rise in the world of judo became a symbol of the country's spirit and determination. The story of those early competitions, of the first Mongolian judo champions, was a story of overcoming obstacles, of blending tradition with innovation, and of a nation proving that even the unlikeliest of underdogs can make their mark on the world stage. The road to becoming judo champions was not an easy one, but the Mongolian judoka of the 1960s and beyond demonstrated that with heart, adaptability, and hard work, anything was possible.

Profiles of early Mongolian Judo pioneers.

In the early days of Mongolian judo, the athletes who stepped forward were more than just competitors—they were pioneers. They were individuals who took the untested steps into a sport that was both foreign and exciting, and they had the courage to push beyond the traditional world of Bökh wrestling into something entirely new. These early Mongolian judo pioneers laid the foundation for the country's future success in the sport, blending the age-old techniques of Mongolian wrestling with the principles of judo. Their stories are marked by resilience, adaptability, and an unyielding sense of national pride.

One of the first names to come up when talking about the early Mongolian judo pioneers is Tsagaanbaatar, who is often considered one of the most important figures in the country's judo history. Born into a family with a history of traditional wrestling, Tsagaanbaatar had the raw athleticism and mental toughness that made him an exceptional candidate for the sport. But judo, unlike the open, expansive fields of Bökh wrestling, was a controlled environment—rules, stances, grips, and techniques that were all new to him.

When Mongolia first began integrating judo into its athletic programs, Tsagaanbaatar was one of the athletes chosen to represent his country. He had never been to an international judo competition before, and his training had largely been focused on traditional Mongolian wrestling. But there was something about his wrestling background that gave him an edge. In Bökh, the key to success was not just strength but balance, timing, and agility. These qualities naturally translated well into judo, which also emphasized using an opponent's momentum and balance against them. Still, the transition from Bökh to judo was not smooth. Tsagaanbaatar had to learn the intricacies of grips, throws, and ground techniques that were foreign to him. He had to adapt quickly, using his instincts and training to keep up with the global judo community, which was much more advanced than Mongolia's fledgling judo scene.

His breakthrough moment came in 1965, when Mongolia made its debut at the World Judo Championships in Paris. Tsagaanbaatar's performance was a revelation. Not only did he hold his own against more seasoned competitors, but he also managed to win a medal, marking the first significant international success for Mongolia in judo. His victory was symbolic—proof that Mongolian wrestlers could adapt their traditional skills to judo and succeed on the world stage. Tsagaanbaatar's win was a turning point for Mongolian judo, a moment that inspired many other athletes to take up the sport seriously.

Alongside Tsagaanbaatar, there was another early judo figure, Bat-Erdene, who became one of the most recognized faces in Mongolian judo. Bat-Erdene's story was one of gradual, steady progress. He started in the early 1960s, when Mongolia was still building its judo infrastructure. Like many of his contemporaries, Bat-Erdene came from a wrestling background. But what set him apart was his dedication to mastering judo's formal techniques, something that would prove to be a crucial advantage in competitions. He spent long hours in the training hall, where he practiced not only the throws but also the more delicate aspects of judo, such as grips and body positioning. While many of his fellow wrestlers adapted their wrestling style directly to judo, Bat-Erdene took the time to learn from Japanese masters and worked hard to understand the subtleties of the sport.

In 1967, Bat-Erdene became one of the first Mongolian judoka to win an international judo competition. His victory was important not just for its significance in the judo community but also for Mongolia's growing pride in the sport. His success was proof that Mongolian athletes, though new to judo, could compete at the highest levels. Bat-Erdene's journey wasn't just about personal triumph; it was about setting an example for others to follow. He showed that success in judo wasn't just about brute strength or natural ability—it was about understanding the sport's philosophy and committing to the training necessary to master it. Bat-Erdene's role in Mongolia's early judo development cannot be overstated. His perseverance and dedication helped pave the way for future generations of judo athletes.

But Tsagaanbaatar and Bat-Erdene weren't the only ones who made their mark. In the early days of Mongolian judo, many athletes, most of them unknown to the international judo community, quietly dedicated themselves to the sport. People like Davaasuren, a judoka known for his rapid progression and exceptional speed, made waves in the local competitions before getting the opportunity to represent Mongolia internationally. His specialty was in foot sweeps and other low-level attacks, which, though unorthodox, had a distinctive Mongolian flavor. His matches were always dramatic, full of intensity, with high-speed exchanges that kept both his opponents and spectators on edge. Although he didn't win major international competitions at first, his contributions to shaping Mongolian judo were undeniable. His style was a mixture of raw athleticism and sheer willpower.

Alongside these men, coaches and mentors who had experience in traditional wrestling played a key role in molding the early judo athletes. One of the most influential figures during this time was Coach Ganbold, a former wrestler who had turned his attention to judo in the late 1950s. His understanding of both Bökh and judo gave him a unique perspective on how the two could be integrated. He trained athletes like Tsagaanbaatar and Bat-Erdene, using his own wrestling expertise to supplement their judo training. Coach Ganbold was known for his unorthodox drills—he would often have the athletes work on maintaining balance and creating leverage, skills that were more commonly associated with wrestling than judo. His methods helped give Mongolian judo a distinct style, characterized by powerful throws and aggressive, fast-paced attacks. Ganbold was not just a coach but a mentor, and his ability to blend the best of both worlds—wrestling and judo—was a crucial factor in the success of his athletes.

As the years passed, the early pioneers of Mongolian judo continued to push the boundaries, and the sport grew in popularity. Tsagaanbaatar, Bat-Erdene, Davaasuren, and Coach Ganbold became legends in their own right, remembered for their contributions to a sport that, when they started, was still foreign and unfamiliar to many. They were not just athletes; they were the foundation of a national judo movement that would, over time, become a force to be reckoned with in international competition. Their stories are not just about winning medals—they are about the spirit of a nation, determined to adapt and overcome, one throw at a time.

Key victories that put Mongolia on the map.

Mongolia's journey into the world of judo wasn't a smooth or predictable one, but there were key moments that helped put the country on the map. These moments weren't just victories; they were turning points that showed the world that Mongolia, with its unique wrestling culture and fierce spirit, could be a force in the international judo arena. It was a series of triumphs, often against the odds, that marked the rise of Mongolia as a judo powerhouse.

The first major victory came in 1965, at the World Judo Championships in Paris. This was the moment when Mongolia, still in the early stages of developing its judo program, made its debut on the international stage. At the time, Mongolia was relatively unknown in the world of judo. The country had a rich tradition of wrestling, but judo was something entirely new. Mongolia's athletes weren't the polished competitors seen in other countries, particularly the Soviet Union or Japan, which had long-established judo programs. Yet, despite the odds stacked against them, Mongolia's athletes brought something to the table that no one had anticipated—a fierce, relentless determination.

Tsagaanbaatar, one of the country's first judo athletes, stood out in this competition. His wrestling background, deeply rooted in Mongolia's centuries-old Bökh tradition, gave him a raw power and agility that his more seasoned opponents were not ready for. Tsagaanbaatar's techniques were not the conventional judo throws that many of the other competitors were familiar with. Instead, he used his wrestling instincts to disrupt his opponents' balance, catching them off guard. His performance at the 1965 World Judo Championships was unexpected, but it was a revelation. Tsagaanbaatar didn't just participate; he impressed. By the end of the tournament, he had won a medal, a historic moment for Mongolia, and an important milestone in the country's judo history. This victory wasn't just personal—it was a victory for the entire nation, showing that Mongolia could hold its own on the world stage. It was the first sign that Mongolia had the potential to be a dominant force in judo.

After that, the momentum only grew. In 1967, Mongolia again competed at the World Judo Championships, and this time, Bat-Erdene—a rising star in the judo community—took center stage. Bat-Erdene was another product of Mongolia's wrestling culture, but he had committed himself to mastering judo's formal techniques. His determination to combine the power of Bökh with the precision of judo made him a unique competitor. He trained tirelessly, pushing himself to understand not only the physical aspects of the sport but also the tactical and mental components. His breakthrough came when he clinched a major international victory in 1967. This was a turning point for Mongolian judo. It wasn't just a personal triumph for Bat-Erdene—it was a statement to the rest of the judo world that Mongolia was no longer just a country with a wrestling history. It was becoming a judo nation, with a style all its own.

In the following years, the success of Tsagaanbaatar and Bat-Erdene inspired more Mongolian athletes to take up judo. There was a palpable sense of excitement and national pride every time a Mongolian athlete stepped onto the mat. But the most significant moment came in 1971, at the World Judo Championships held in Ludwigshafen, Germany. This was a year when Mongolia sent a full team, and the world would see that the country had developed into a serious contender. The athletes, led by the seasoned veterans and newcomers alike, were prepared. They had refined their techniques and were now ready to face the toughest judo practitioners in the world.

It was during this competition that Mongolia truly announced its arrival. A young judoka named Davaasuren stunned the judo community by taking home a gold medal. His victory wasn't just about technical skill, although he had that in abundance—it was about his heart, his will, and his ability to adapt under pressure. Davaasuren was known for his speed and agility, traits that served him well in judo. He used his low center of gravity, a characteristic of many Mongolian wrestlers, to outmaneuver his opponents, often catching them off balance with swift, unexpected throws. His gold medal at the 1971 World Judo Championships was monumental. It was the first time Mongolia had won a gold medal in an international judo competition, and it cemented the country's place on the global judo map.

Davaasuren's victory wasn't just important for Mongolia; it marked a shift in the way the international judo community viewed the country. No longer was Mongolia an outsider, struggling to make its presence known. With this gold medal, Mongolia had become a legitimate threat. This was the turning point where Mongolia stopped being seen as the underdog and began to be feared as a real contender in the world of judo.

The ripple effect of Davaasuren's victory spread throughout Mongolia. It sparked an even greater interest in judo. Athletes from all walks of life began to see the sport not just as a foreign discipline but as something that could be uniquely Mongolian. They began to embrace the idea that Mongolian wrestling could be integrated into judo, creating a distinctive style that was both unpredictable and effective. Young judoka, inspired by Davaasuren's success, began flocking to training centers, eager to develop their skills and represent Mongolia on the world stage.

Following that gold medal in 1971, Mongolia's judo athletes continued to shine. They began to appear regularly in the later stages of international competitions, and their success was no longer a matter of luck but a result of years of hard work and dedication. The country's judo program was no longer in its infancy—it had grown into a mature, competitive force.

These victories—the breakthrough moments in 1965, 1967, and the gold medal in 1971—were not just about individual accomplishments. They were about the growth of a sport that was still young in Mongolia. They represented the merging of tradition and modernity, of old wrestling techniques being reshaped into a new form. The victories were the result of a shared effort—a community that came together to prove that they could not only participate but excel in a global sport. Each victory was a step forward, each one confirming that Mongolia had a place in the world of judo. And over time, that place became more and more secure. The world had begun to take notice, and Mongolia, once a newcomer to judo, was now a nation to be reckoned with.

Chapter 8: The 2008 Olympic Breakthrough

The story of Naidangiin Tüvshinbayar, Mongolia's first Olympic gold medalist in Judo.

In the summer of 2008, a moment unfolded that would forever change the trajectory of Mongolian judo. It wasn't just a victory—it was a dream realized, a historic breakthrough that solidified Mongolia's place among the elite in international sports. The man at the center of this moment was Naidangiin Tüvshinbayar, Mongolia's first Olympic gold medalist in judo, and his story is one of perseverance, passion, and pride.

For Tüvshinbayar, the journey to the Olympic stage began many years before that fateful summer in Beijing. Growing up in the small town of Töv, he was introduced to wrestling at an early age, much like many Mongolian children. Wrestling, part of the national identity, was in his blood. But as he got older, Tüvshinbayar's aspirations expanded beyond the familiar mats of traditional Bökh wrestling. He wanted more. He sought a new challenge, something that could combine the raw power of wrestling with the technical demands of a globally recognized sport. Judo, with its emphasis on balance, timing, and throws, became his calling.

The transition from Mongolian wrestling to judo was not easy. The two sports may have shared some similarities, but judo's rules, its structure, and its techniques were foreign. In the beginning, Tüvshinbayar struggled. He had the strength, yes, but he lacked the finesse required for judo. He had to adjust his thinking—how to use an opponent's force against them, how to execute throws with precision, and how to engage in groundwork that was far more complex than what he had known. But Tüvshinbayar wasn't one to back down from a challenge. He trained relentlessly, often pushing himself to the brink of exhaustion. His coaches, understanding the potential in him, worked tirelessly to refine his technique. Over time, the raw power of his wrestling background began to merge with the precision of judo, and he started to shine.

In the years leading up to the 2008 Beijing Olympics, Tüvshinbayar had already made a name for himself in the international judo community. He had won numerous regional titles and competed at the World Judo Championships, gaining valuable experience. Yet, despite his success, there was one goal that had eluded him: an Olympic gold medal. For a nation as small as Mongolia, the Olympics were an immense stage. The hopes and dreams of an entire country rested on the shoulders of a few athletes, and Tüvshinbayar knew this. But he was ready.

By the time the 2008 Olympics rolled around, he had already proven himself to be a formidable competitor. He was in peak condition, mentally and physically prepared, and the stage was set for something monumental. When he entered the competition, the world was watching. Tüvshinbayar was in the 100kg weight category, and the judo competition was fierce. Among his opponents were some of the best athletes in the world—judo giants from countries like France, Japan, and Brazil. But Tüvshinbayar wasn't intimidated. His training had sharpened him into a weapon—calculating, determined, and driven by a deep sense of national pride.

The first few rounds of the competition were tense. Tüvshinbayar's opponents were skilled, and every match seemed to be a battle of wills. But Tüvshinbayar's resolve never faltered. In each contest, he showcased a blend of Mongolian wrestling tactics and judo expertise. His throws were powerful, his grips tight, and his movements efficient. As he advanced through the rounds, it became clear: he wasn't just competing; he was dominating.

And then came the final. Tüvshinbayar faced off against the French judoka, Teddy Riner, a towering figure in the world of judo who had been undefeated for years. Riner, who stood at over two meters tall and weighed more than Tüvshinbayar, was a formidable opponent. He was the reigning world champion and the favorite to win gold. But Tüvshinbayar wasn't concerned with Riner's reputation. His focus was unshakeable, his determination clear. He had come this far, and there was no turning back.

The final match was a stunning display of skill and strength. Both fighters were evenly matched, each trying to outmaneuver the other with a series of throws, grips, and counters. But as the match wore on, it became evident that Tüvshinbayar's speed and agility were giving him an edge. In the last seconds of the match, with both competitors exhausted, Tüvshinbayar found an opening. With a swift movement, he executed a perfect throw, sending Riner to the mat. The crowd erupted into applause as Tüvshinbayar stood over his opponent, the realization of his victory slowly sinking in. He had done it. He had beaten the best in the world and claimed Mongolia's first-ever Olympic gold medal in judo.

When Tüvshinbayar stood on the podium, the Mongolian flag raised above him, and the national anthem played, it wasn't just a personal victory. It was a victory for Mongolia itself. For a small country with a proud wrestling tradition but no real history in judo, this moment was everything. The streets of Ulaanbaatar erupted in celebration. Mongolians, who had watched with bated breath as their hero competed, poured into the streets in jubilation. Tüvshinbayar's win wasn't just a triumph of athleticism; it was a testament to the spirit of a nation. It showed that with hard work, dedication, and a belief in one's own abilities, even the smallest nations could make a mark on the world.

In the years since, Tüvshinbayar has become a symbol of Mongolian pride and perseverance. His victory at the 2008 Olympics is remembered as one of the most significant moments in the history of Mongolian sports. He continues to inspire generations of young athletes, not just in judo, but in every sport. His success demonstrated that with passion and commitment, dreams that once seemed impossible could become a reality. For Mongolian judo, the 2008 Olympics marked a turning point—a moment that cemented the country's place among the best in the world. And for Tüvshinbayar, it was the fulfillment of a lifelong dream and a moment of national glory that will never be forgotten.

How this victory inspired a new generation of athletes.

The 2008 Olympic gold medal win by Naidangiin Tüvshinbayar wasn't just a moment of personal triumph; it was a watershed event for Mongolian sports as a whole. When Tüvshinbayar stood on that podium in Beijing, the sense of pride and joy that spread across Mongolia was nothing short of overwhelming. This victory was a culmination of years of hard work, a moment where all the hopes and dreams of a small nation were realized. It wasn't just about one man's achievement; it was about the rise of a whole country, a nation that had long been known for its wrestling traditions but had never tasted the sweet success of Olympic gold in judo. Tüvshinbayar's victory marked a turning point, one that would leave a deep and lasting impact on Mongolian sports and inspire an entirely new generation of athletes.

For Mongolia, sports were more than just games; they were an integral part of the national identity. Wrestling, especially the traditional form known as Bökh, had long been the sport of the people. Generations had grown up learning the art of wrestling, and it was woven into the very fabric of the culture. But when Tüvshinbayar clinched that gold medal in judo, something profound happened. It wasn't just a shift in sports; it was a shift in mindset. Mongolia, for so long tied to its ancient wrestling roots, suddenly saw the potential to excel in other sports too.

Tüvshinbayar's victory had a ripple effect that spread far beyond the judo mats. The entire country seemed to rise in celebration, from the bustling streets of Ulaanbaatar to the quieter corners of the countryside. People who had never paid attention to judo before now followed the sport with intense interest. For the first time, Mongolians believed they could achieve greatness not just in wrestling, but in other arenas of sports on the global stage.

The impact on the national psyche was immeasurable. Tüvshinbayar was hailed as a hero, not only for his athleticism but for his role in inspiring pride and confidence in his people. His gold medal became a symbol of what Mongolia could achieve if it set its mind to something. It wasn't just about judo—it was about what was possible when a nation came together to support its athletes, when the collective spirit of a country was harnessed for a common purpose. The victory was a beacon of hope, showing that no matter how small or remote a nation might be, it could compete with the giants of the world and succeed.

But perhaps the most significant legacy of Tüvshinbayar's victory was the way it inspired a new generation of athletes. Young people across Mongolia began to see sports in a new light. They were no longer just training for traditional wrestling matches; they were now dreaming of Olympic glory in a wide variety of sports. Tüvshinbayar

128

showed them that anything was possible. His victory proved that if they worked hard enough, if they honed their skills and stayed disciplined, they too could make their mark on the world. The gold medal was a call to action, a message to the youth that they had the potential to become champions in their own right.

From schools to local judo clubs, Tüvshinbayar's success created a surge of interest in judo, particularly among young Mongolian athletes. Boys and girls alike started flocking to judo dojos, inspired by the idea that their country had a chance to become a judo powerhouse. The younger generation, many of whom had once idolized wrestlers, now had new role models to look up to—athletes who had risen through the ranks of judo and made history.

But the ripple effects of Tüvshinbayar's victory weren't limited to judo alone. Other sports also saw a boost in interest and participation. Football, basketball, and athletics all began to see an influx of talent, as young people now believed that success in these sports, too, was achievable. Tüvshinbayar's Olympic gold provided proof that a Mongolian athlete could excel on the global stage, and that made all the difference. It was no longer enough to just follow tradition. The younger generation began to realize that they could break out, that they could forge their own paths and compete at the highest levels.

In the years following Tüvshinbayar's win, Mongolia witnessed a surge of new athletes breaking through in various disciplines. These were young men and women who, inspired by Tüvshinbayar's story, decided to take up sports seriously and dedicate themselves to the pursuit of excellence. More Mongolian athletes began making their mark at the Asian Games, World Championships, and even in the Olympics. Tüvshinbayar's victory had ignited a fire, one that was spreading fast and turning Mongolia into a nation known not just for its wrestling but for its growing influence in other sports as well.

Moreover, Tüvshinbayar's win helped establish a greater sense of unity in the country. The pride that came with his victory transcended regional divides and brought people from all walks of life together. For a brief moment, it seemed that Mongolia, despite its struggles and hardships, had something to celebrate—a shared achievement that united the entire nation.

The rise in national pride wasn't just about the victory itself, but about what it represented. Tüvshinbayar's gold medal was the physical manifestation of the hard work, the sacrifices, and the dream of a country that had long been overlooked in the international sports arena. His success meant that Mongolia had truly arrived on the world stage, and the nation could no longer be ignored. This victory showed that with determination, unity, and the right opportunities, Mongolia could compete with the best.

In the years that followed, Tüvshinbayar remained a revered figure in Mongolia. He continued to inspire not just athletes but anyone who dared to dream big. The effects of his historic win were felt for generations, and his legacy endured in the young athletes who, because of him, believed that anything was possible. Tüvshinbayar showed them the way, and for Mongolia, his victory was just the beginning of a new chapter—one filled with hope, pride, and the promise of more victories to come.

Chapter 9: The Modern Era of Mongolian Judo

Mongolia's ongoing success in international Judo competitions

Since Naidangiin Tüvshinbayar's groundbreaking Olympic victory in 2008, Mongolia's judo scene has evolved into a formidable force on the international stage. That moment of glory, when Tüvshinbayar stood atop the podium in Beijing, wasn't just a flash of brilliance—it was the spark that ignited an era of success for Mongolian judo. Today, Mongolia is known for producing top-level judo athletes, and the country's judo story continues to unfold with pride and determination.

In the years following Tüvshinbayar's win, Mongolia's presence in judo competitions around the world has grown steadily. The country has made its mark at multiple global tournaments, including the World Judo Championships and the Asian Games, earning medals and respect. What began as a dream, catalyzed by one man's historic achievement, has blossomed into a movement that is now deeply ingrained in the country's sports culture. Judo has become a sport of national importance, one that attracts young talent from all corners of Mongolia, driven by the hope of following in Tüvshinbayar's footsteps.

Mongolian judo has gained recognition for its aggressive style, a blend of power, speed, and technique that reflects both the wrestling traditions of the country and the strategic approach of judo. The country's judoka have continued to excel, showing up at international competitions with intensity, determination, and a clear sense of pride in their heritage. They fight with a spirit that comes from knowing that they represent more than just themselves—they carry the weight of a nation's expectations.

One of the key factors behind Mongolia's ongoing success in judo is the country's dedication to developing talent from a young age. Since the early days following Tüvshinbayar's Olympic victory, there has been a concerted effort to build judo infrastructure throughout Mongolia. Judo schools and training camps have flourished, with young athletes enrolling in specialized programs to hone their skills. Coaches, many of whom are former athletes, have been instrumental in nurturing the next generation of champions. These athletes train hard, often in conditions that would seem tough to outsiders, but it's precisely this environment that has created a culture of resilience and grit.

Mongolian judo has also benefitted from the support of the government and various sports organizations. There has been an investment in developing judo facilities and bringing in international expertise to improve training methods. The government has recognized that success in international competitions not only brings pride to the country but also elevates its international standing. The support from the public and private sectors has enabled Mongolia to send more athletes to international tournaments and provide them with the resources they need to succeed.

Since Tüvshinbayar's triumph, Mongolia has continued to produce outstanding judoka who have excelled at the highest levels. Athletes like Munkhbat, who earned a bronze medal at the 2012 London Olympics, and the rising star, Urantsetseg Munkhbat, who made history by winning medals at the World Judo Championships, have carried the flag high. These athletes have shown that Tüvshinbayar's success wasn't just a fluke, but the start of a new era for Mongolian judo. Each victory has reinforced the belief that Mongolia can compete with the world's best, and the hunger for more success grows with each passing year.

Urantsetseg Munkhbat's career, in particular, stands as a testament to the persistence and passion that now defines Mongolian judo. She's not only one of the top-ranked female judoka in her weight class, but she's also become a symbol of the country's growth in the sport. Her performances on the international stage have helped elevate the profile of Mongolian judo even further. When she won her silver medal at the 2020 Tokyo Olympics, it wasn't just a personal triumph—it was another milestone for Mongolia, further solidifying the nation's place on the global judo map.

Yet, success in judo is not just measured in medals and rankings. It's about the spirit of the athletes, the relentless pursuit of excellence, and the deep-rooted belief that anything is possible. The young judoka of Mongolia, many of whom come from humble backgrounds, continue to chase their dreams with a fervor that's hard to ignore. They know that each match they fight is not just for a medal, but for a place in the legacy of Mongolian judo. These athletes often train in small, crowded gyms, with limited resources, but what they lack in material wealth, they more than make up for in heart and determination.

Mongolian judo has also seen a shift in the way it interacts with the world. The country's athletes are no longer just hopeful competitors; they are now feared opponents. The legacy of Tüvshinbayar's victory has put Mongolian judo on the radar of top-tier judo nations, and every time a Mongolian judoka steps onto the mat, they carry the weight of the country's pride. Their fierce, unrelenting style has earned them respect from the global judo community, and with each new success, Mongolia's reputation continues to grow.

Looking ahead, the future of Mongolian judo seems brighter than ever. The next generation of athletes is already making waves, and the pipeline of young talent continues to expand. More and more children are entering judo clubs, inspired by the heroes who have come before them. The next Naidangiin Tüvshinbayar may already be training in a gym somewhere in Mongolia, working tirelessly to achieve the same level of greatness. And with the continued support of the Mongolian people and a robust system of development, there's every reason to believe that the country's judo successes will only continue to grow.

Mongolia's rise in the judo world is a story of transformation, a story of a small country punching far above its weight, driven by the passion of its people and the legacy of its champions. From Tüvshinbayar's historic gold medal to the rising stars of today, Mongolian judo has become a force to be reckoned with on the global stage. And as the nation continues to build on its successes, the world will be watching, knowing that Mongolia's best may still be yet to come.

Profiles of contemporary champions and rising stars.

Mongolian judo, after decades of building strength and international respect, is now home to some of the world's most formidable judoka. These athletes, through their grit and determination, have become symbols of the country's growing prowess on the global stage. Their stories are rooted in sacrifice, hard work, and a relentless desire to honor their homeland. As the new generation of Mongolian judoka rises, they carry forward the legacy of those who have come before them, each athlete carving out their own place in history.

One of the most notable figures in Mongolian judo today is Urantsetseg Munkhbat. She has not just carried the flag of Mongolian judo—she's helped redefine what the country can achieve in the sport. Munkhbat's career has been nothing short of extraordinary. Born and raised in the small town of Altai, in the western part of Mongolia, she grew up with the kind of toughness and resilience that has become the hallmark of Mongolian athletes. From a young age, it was clear she had a natural talent for judo. But it wasn't just talent that propelled her to the top—it was her unwavering determination and ability to push herself past every limit.

Munkhbat's breakthrough came at the 2016 Rio Olympics, where she won a bronze medal, becoming one of the few Mongolian women to achieve such a feat on the world's biggest stage. Her victory wasn't just about athletic achievement—it was a moment that reinforced the growing strength of Mongolian judo. She became a household name, a role model for young girls and boys across Mongolia, showing them that greatness was possible, no matter where they came from. But it was her silver medal in the 2020 Tokyo Olympics that truly cemented her status as one of Mongolia's best. To win silver, in the face of the world's top athletes, was a testament to Munkhbat's perseverance and focus.

Her career continues to inspire the next generation of Mongolian judoka. Young athletes in the streets of Ulaanbaatar and in the rural corners of the country now have a female champion to look up to. Munkhbat's story proves that with discipline and heart, an athlete can make an impact far beyond their home country. Her accomplishments show that Mongolia is no longer just about traditional wrestling; it's a nation that can excel across the sporting world, and Urantsetseg Munkhbat is living proof of that.

Another rising star who has garnered attention in recent years is Ganzorig Ganbat. Known for his explosive power and unrelenting style, Ganbat has quickly made a name for himself on the international judo scene. His raw talent was evident early on, and it didn't take long for him to rise through the ranks. His aggressive approach to judo has often caught his opponents off guard, earning him victories in some of the most competitive tournaments in Asia and Europe. He's a fighter who never gives up, always pressing forward, no matter the odds. Ganbat has been touted as one of the athletes who could carry Mongolian judo to even greater heights in the years to come.

Ganbat's most notable achievement came at the 2021 World Judo Championships, where he won a gold medal, marking a historic moment for Mongolia. The victory was not just a personal triumph for Ganbat; it was another indication that Mongolia's dominance in judo was no fluke. The country's judoka were here to stay, and their victories were beginning to pile up. Ganbat's win was celebrated not only by his teammates and coaches but by the entire nation. It reminded everyone that while the country may be small, its athletes were capable of competing at the very highest level.

Then there's the rising star of the 60 kg division, Tumurkhuleg Otgonbaatar. At just 23, Tumurkhuleg is already considered one of the most promising talents in Mongolian judo. His combination of speed, technique, and mental toughness has earned him multiple national titles and a growing reputation on the international circuit. Tumurkhuleg has steadily been climbing the rankings in his weight class, competing in major tournaments across Asia and Europe. His raw potential is clear, and many believe he could be the next big name to bring home a medal from the Olympics or World Championships.

What makes Tumurkhuleg's rise particularly exciting is the humility and discipline with which he carries himself. Like so many of

Mongolia's top athletes, he knows the road to the top is paved with sacrifice. He trains in the early hours of the morning, pushing his body to its limits while staying focused on his long-term goals. His commitment is unwavering, and it's clear that he's prepared to work for every victory that comes his way. His ambition isn't just to win medals—it's to elevate Mongolian judo to even greater heights, to build on the foundation laid by those who came before him.

Alongside these established and rising stars, there are countless other athletes emerging from Mongolia's judo system, each with their own potential to make an impact. The growth of judo in Mongolia is no longer a story of individual success—it's a story of collective achievement. The success of athletes like Munkhbat, Ganbat, and Tumurkhuleg has created an environment where young judoka can dream big, knowing that they have role models to follow. The country's investment in judo infrastructure and youth development has created a pipeline of talent that will continue to produce champions for years to come.

But what truly sets Mongolian judo apart is the spirit of its athletes. These competitors aren't just training for themselves; they're training for their country, for their families, and for the generations that will follow them. There's a sense of pride in their work ethic, a pride that can't be replicated on any other mat in the world. Each time a Mongolian judoka steps into an international competition, they know they carry the hopes of a nation with them. And that pressure? It's what fuels them to go further, to fight harder, and to achieve greatness.

Mongolian judo is a force to be reckoned with, and the athletes leading the way today are proof that the country's success in the sport is no accident. From the seasoned veterans like Munkhbat to the rising stars like Ganbat and Tumurkhuleg, the future of Mongolian judo looks brighter than ever. These athletes are not just making history—they are continuing a legacy, one that will inspire generations of Mongolian judoka for years to come. The journey of Mongolian judo is far from over, and with these athletes leading the charge, the world should be ready for even more incredible victories.

How Mongolia continues to innovate and influence the global Judo scene.

Mongolia's influence on the global judo scene has expanded far beyond its humble beginnings. What started as a country slowly carving out its place in the sport has grown into a powerhouse that not only competes at the highest levels but also innovates in ways that continue to shape the future of judo. Today, Mongolia is no longer just a competitor; it's a trendsetter. From the unique style of its athletes to its revolutionary approach to training, Mongolia has become a key player in the global judo community, and the world is taking notice.

It all began with the rise of judo stars like Naidangiin Tüvshinbayar and Urantsetseg Munkhbat, whose Olympic medals put Mongolia on the map. But it didn't stop there. Their victories were the foundation upon which a new era of judo was built in Mongolia. Young athletes, inspired by the feats of their predecessors, began to pour into judo clubs across the country. What set them apart wasn't just their skill—it was the intensity with which they trained, and the deep understanding of the sport's roots mixed with Mongolia's traditional wrestling culture. Mongolia's judo style, often characterized by a fierce, no-holds-barred approach, quickly became recognized internationally as unique and formidable.

One of the most significant ways Mongolia continues to innovate in judo is through its ability to blend the ancient techniques of Bökh, the

142

country's traditional form of wrestling, with the more technical aspects of judo. Bökh is a sport deeply embedded in Mongolian culture, and it's one that demands a high degree of physical strength, balance, and mental focus. These qualities translate well into judo, where the emphasis is on using an opponent's force against them. Mongolian judoka have developed a reputation for their aggressive, yet controlled, fighting style, often surprising their opponents with unexpected moves. This fusion of old and new has given Mongolian judo a distinct edge, one that's difficult to replicate.

Beyond technique, Mongolia's approach to training is another area where innovation shines. The country has developed a unique system for scouting and nurturing talent. Unlike many nations, where young athletes are often funneled into specialized sports programs from an early age, Mongolia's judo system focuses on broad athletic development. Kids who show promise in any form of wrestling or martial arts are often introduced to judo, where they can refine their skills and learn new techniques. This versatility in training is one of the reasons why Mongolian judoka tend to adapt quickly to different styles, often giving them an advantage when competing internationally. They are trained to be flexible and adaptable, able to adjust their strategy in real-time to outsmart opponents.

Mongolian athletes are also known for their resilience and mental toughness—qualities that are deeply rooted in the country's history of surviving in some of the harshest environments on earth. The nation's struggle against foreign powers, its nomadic traditions, and its fierce pride in self-reliance have fostered an unyielding spirit in its people. This mental fortitude is what sets Mongolian judoka apart from the rest of the world. The country's athletes train in tough conditions, often with limited resources, but this very environment creates an iron will that drives them to succeed, no matter the circumstances. This sense of national pride and determination is palpable when watching Mongolian judoka compete—there's always an intensity in their eyes that shows they are fighting for something greater than themselves.

On the international stage, Mongolia's impact is undeniable. The nation's success in judo competitions, from the Olympics to the World Championships, has forced the global community to take notice. But Mongolia's influence extends beyond its victories. The country's judoka have changed the way the world thinks about the sport, especially in terms of strategy and approach. Where many nations focus on pure technique and precision, Mongolian judoka bring a raw, physical style that's rooted in the concept of "throwing everything into the fight." This style—aggressive and full of energy—has given rise to a new way of thinking about judo, one that blends technique with brute strength in ways that haven't always been explored by other nations.

In addition to the fighting style, the Mongolian way of training has influenced other judo systems around the world. Coaches from Japan, Russia, and Europe have begun to incorporate elements of Mongolian training techniques into their own programs, especially the emphasis on resilience and adaptability. There is a growing recognition that judo isn't just about perfecting throws and holds; it's also about mental toughness, aggression, and the willingness to embrace unconventional methods when necessary. Mongolia's success in these areas has paved the way for a more diverse and dynamic approach to the sport, one that values the unpredictable as much as the planned.

One of the more striking innovations in Mongolian judo is how the country has maintained its close ties to the past while embracing the modern evolution of the sport. The blend of Bökh-inspired moves with Olympic judo techniques has created a hybrid style that is uniquely Mongolian. This approach has not only proved successful in competitions but has also inspired a wave of new techniques and strategies. Mongolian judoka are often seen experimenting with new grips, throws, and ground game tactics that surprise their competitors. This willingness to innovate, combined with a respect for tradition, has helped Mongolia maintain its position as a global force in judo.

Looking forward, Mongolia's influence on the global judo scene will likely continue to grow. As more and more young athletes rise through the ranks, the country's impact on the sport is only set to increase. Mongolia's dedication to developing homegrown talent, its unique fusion of old and new techniques, and its unbreakable spirit have made it a leader in judo innovation. Whether it's through the success of individual athletes or the country's evolving judo culture, Mongolia's presence on the international stage is not just a flash in the pan—it's a legacy in the making. The world will continue to watch, and Mongolia will continue to inspire.

Chapter 10: Bökh Wrestling and Judo Philosophy

The shared values of strength, respect, and perseverance.

In the world of combat sports, the lines between different traditions often blur. In Mongolia, that blur is particularly strong between judo and Bökh wrestling. Though they are distinct, these two sports share core values that have become fundamental to Mongolian culture: strength, respect, and perseverance. These values aren't just for the mat—they're philosophies that permeate every aspect of life in Mongolia. To understand how judo and Bökh are connected, it's essential to first appreciate the deep-rooted principles that guide them both.

Sukhbaatar, a seasoned judo coach who has seen generations of athletes come and go, sat down with a young group of judoka in a small gym in Ulaanbaatar. The air was thick with the sound of bodies hitting mats, the sharp breath of athletes grappling for dominance. Sukhbaatar, a former wrestler who had transitioned to coaching judo, often began his sessions with stories—stories of his childhood, of training under harsh conditions, of watching Mongolian wrestlers carry the pride of the nation on their shoulders. He believed that the mental discipline of Bökh was the foundation of a strong judo mindset.

"It's about strength," he said one day, his voice steady and commanding. "But not just physical strength. Strength of spirit. That's what separates the great from the good. The same strength that keeps a wrestler grounded, when the world wants to throw them off balance, is the same strength a judoka needs when the odds seem impossible."

The room fell silent as his words settled. Young athletes who had only known the controlled chaos of judo now saw it through a new lens. They weren't just learning how to throw or pin an opponent; they were learning how to endure, how to stand firm in the face of adversity.

In many ways, Mongolian judo and Bökh are two sides of the same coin. The throws and grappling techniques in both sports require precise body control, an understanding of leverage, and an awareness of timing. But it's the mental fortitude that is at the heart of both. The values of Bökh—honor, resilience, and respect—are the bedrock on which Mongolian judo has built its reputation. The idea that a competitor must not only be physically strong but also morally steadfast is one that has been passed down through generations.

An older wrestler, Bat-Erdene, sat quietly in the back of the gym, watching the young judoka with a thoughtful expression. Bat-Erdene had competed in the traditional Mongolian wrestling tournaments before transitioning to coaching, and he saw the sport differently than most. For him, Bökh was not just a fight for dominance; it was a spiritual journey.

He spoke to the group one afternoon, his voice rough but earnest. "In Bökh, there's a phrase we often use—'Zaluu erguul', which means 'you are only as strong as your ability to recover.' It's not about how many times you fall; it's about how many times you get back up." His eyes scanned the young athletes. "In judo, you must have that same mentality. You will fall. You will fail. But it's in those moments that you truly become who you are meant to be."

His words echoed through the gym, lingering in the minds of the judoka. The idea of resilience—that a fighter's true strength is revealed not in their victories but in their ability to rise after defeat—was a lesson they would carry with them into every match. It wasn't just about winning; it was about facing the hardships of the fight and standing tall, no matter the result.

Respect, too, was a core tenet that tied Bökh and judo together. This value was visible in the way athletes greeted each other before and after a match—bowing, a tradition that had been passed down from generation to generation. In the world of both judo and Bökh, the mat was sacred, and the respect for one's opponent was paramount.

One day, as part of his training, Sukhbaatar paired off with a young athlete named Munkh-Erdene, a rising star who had recently joined the national team. The two were going through a series of sparring drills, their bodies moving with practiced precision, the sounds of their throws echoing in the gym. After a particularly tough session, Munkh-Erdene, exhausted and bruised, turned to Sukhbaatar.

"I feel like I'm not getting it," he said, sweat dripping down his face. "I keep losing my balance, and I don't know how to correct it."

Sukhbaatar, wiping his forehead, smiled and placed a hand on Munkh-Erdene's shoulder. "It's not about getting it right every time. It's about learning from every mistake. In judo, like in life, there is no perfect way. There is only the way that works in the moment. Bökh teaches us that. You learn to accept that you will fall, but you will rise again. Each time you rise, you become stronger."

Munkh-Erdene nodded, the weight of Sukhbaatar's words settling in. It was in those quiet moments of guidance that the true nature of judo and Bökh became clear to him. It wasn't just about the sport—it was about growing as a person. It was about pushing yourself, not to defeat others, but to defeat your own limits, your own doubts, your own fears.

As the years passed, Munkh-Erdene's skills grew. He made his way to the international judo circuit, where he would face some of the world's best. But every time he stepped onto the mat, he carried with him the principles of strength, respect, and perseverance that had been instilled in him from his earliest days of training.

Mongolian judo has always been more than a sport—it is a philosophy of life. From the wrestlers of the steppes to the judoka of today, the teachings of Bökh have shaped an entire generation of
150

athletes who approach the world with the same values: the strength to endure, the respect for others, and the perseverance to rise every time they fall.

Sukhbaatar's words, Bat-Erdene's wisdom, and the silent lessons taught through sweat and struggle are a testament to how these traditions live on. For the athletes of Mongolia, judo is not just about mastering techniques—it's about mastering the art of life itself. And in this shared philosophy of strength, respect, and perseverance, judo and Bökh are not just sports—they are ways of living, deeply connected to the very soul of Mongolia.

The blending of Japanese Judo philosophy with Mongolian cultural principles..

In the heart of Asia, where the winds carry the echoes of ancient traditions, the paths of Japanese Judo and Mongolian culture unexpectedly converge, offering a profound and remarkable blend of philosophies. The story of this connection is not just one of combat or technique but of deep-rooted wisdom that transcends borders. Let me take you back to the moments in history where these two cultures, seemingly distant in their practices, found a common ground in their shared values.

Japan, known for its rich martial arts history, has always revered discipline, respect, and the art of peaceful resolution. Judo, born from the mind of Jigoro Kano in the late 19th century, was designed not just as a physical art but as a way of life. It wasn't merely about strength or technique—it was a philosophy that sought to develop the body and mind in unison. Kano's teachings were grounded in the idea of mutual welfare and benefit, focusing on efficiency and balance, on using the opponent's energy rather than opposing it. Judo's principles taught that victory didn't just lie in defeating an opponent, but in the mental and spiritual growth that came from the struggle.

On the other side of Asia, nestled within the vast plains of Mongolia, there was an entirely different but equally powerful philosophy in play. Mongolian culture, with its nomadic roots, had long honored the spirit of resilience, self-reliance, and respect for nature. The Mongolian warrior, often seen atop horseback, was not just a fighter but a symbol of endurance and loyalty to their people. Their wrestling tradition, known as Bökh, has been practiced for centuries. More than just a sport, it embodies the essence of power, agility, and wisdom. The art of Bökh isn't just about physical prowess—it is about understanding one's inner strength, building character, and showing humility in both victory and defeat.

It's fascinating to see how Judo and Mongolian wrestling, while so different in execution, converge on a deeper level. Both arts focus on balance and leverage. In Judo, practitioners learn how to throw an opponent with minimal effort, using the opponent's movements to their advantage. Similarly, in Mongolian wrestling, success often comes not from sheer strength but from the ability to read the opponent's moves, anticipating and reacting with precision. The Mongolian wrestler's philosophy is one of yielding, not always fighting back directly but waiting for the perfect moment to strike, much like a cat preparing to pounce.

But the convergence between Judo and Mongolian culture goes beyond physical technique. There is an unmistakable focus on respect in both traditions. In Judo, this respect is symbolized by bowing before a match, acknowledging the opponent as an equal. Kano's principle of "Seiryoku Zenyo," or maximum efficiency with minimum effort, mirrors the Mongolian ethos of "Batlan," which emphasizes doing what is necessary with the least amount of force or excess. Both cultures value the concept of harmony—whether it is the harmony of the mind and body in Judo or the harmony between a warrior and the natural world in Mongolia.

The mental aspect of Judo finds an echo in Mongolian values as well. In both traditions, there's a deep sense of discipline, a rigorous commitment to constant self-improvement. In the Mongolian warrior culture, there is a saying, "The battle is not won in the field; it is won in the mind." Likewise, Judo is as much about mental fortitude as it is about physical ability. Kano often said that Judo was a way to "make a better society," teaching its practitioners to think not only about victory in combat but about victory in life.

As these traditions evolved, they began to influence one another. In the modern world, there are subtle yet significant exchanges between Judo and Mongolian wrestling, particularly in the context of martial arts competitions. Mongolian wrestlers, who once relied purely on traditional methods, have incorporated elements of Judo's grappling techniques, while Judo practitioners have found inspiration in the patience and timing of Mongolian fighters. The blending of these two martial arts has led to a new understanding of combat—a fusion of efficiency and strength, flexibility and power.

Imagine a Mongolian wrestler stepping onto a Judo mat. He would know how to read his opponent's body language, sensing their weakness even before they make a move. But the Judo practitioner, with his emphasis on balance and leverage, would be prepared to use the wrestler's own force against him. The Mongolian wrestler, with his silent and strategic approach, might be in awe of the fluidity and precision with which Judo is practiced. Similarly, the Judo practitioner might find in the Mongolian warrior's grit and endurance a new sense of inner strength.

It's not just on the mat that these philosophies cross paths. The cultural exchange also brings about a blending of attitudes toward life itself. The Mongolian concept of "Zorig," or courage, aligns with Judo's principle of "Kodokan," the way of training oneself. Both philosophies share an understanding that true strength comes from one's ability to overcome adversity, both in combat and in life. This kind of strength is quiet, unassuming, but undeniable.

Over time, this fusion of Japanese and Mongolian traditions has come to represent something much greater than just two fighting styles. It is the embodiment of a universal truth that stretches across cultures: that true mastery is not just about defeating others, but about understanding and improving oneself. Judo, with its focus on mutual respect and personal growth, and Mongolian culture, with its emphasis on resilience and humility, together offer a powerful blueprint for living. It is not the outcome of the battle that matters most, but the journey—the lessons learned, the strength gained, and the wisdom found along the way.

This blending of philosophies, though born out of different worlds, reveals the shared human pursuit of harmony, balance, and self-mastery. And it is in this shared pursuit that the beauty of both Judo and Mongolian culture lies—two ancient traditions that, in their own ways, teach us that the greatest victory is the one we achieve over ourselves.

Chapter 11: The Role of Coaches and Mentors

Key figures in Mongolia's Judo development.

In the world of martial arts, the role of a coach or mentor cannot be overstated. These figures are more than just instructors; they are the guiding forces that shape the trajectory of athletes, not only teaching them the technicalities of the sport but also imparting lessons that extend far beyond the mat. This is particularly true in Mongolia, where the development of Judo has been deeply intertwined with the wisdom and influence of key mentors and coaches.

Mongolia's rise in Judo is a story of perseverance, vision, and a deep commitment to the idea that success doesn't come easily—it must be nurtured. The country's Judo journey began with a few brave souls who sought to bring the art from Japan to the steppes of Mongolia, where wrestling was already a revered tradition. But it wasn't just the physical aspect of Judo that needed to be taught—it was the philosophy, the respect for the art, and the mental discipline that came with it. That's where the mentors came in.

In Mongolia, Judo took root with the help of individuals who were willing to push boundaries and go beyond traditional practices. The first generation of Judo coaches faced many obstacles. They had to convince their students that Judo was not merely a sport of strength but of balance, technique, and mental resilience. It was a hard sell in a country where wrestling had long been the dominant form of combat and where traditional methods were deeply ingrained. But the coaches were patient. They were driven by a vision of Mongolia not just participating in Judo competitions but excelling on the global stage.

One of the most influential figures in Mongolia's Judo history was Judo pioneer and coach, Ts. Jigjidsuren, who is often credited with being the father of modern Judo in Mongolia. He saw the potential in his students and understood that to compete with the world's best, Mongolian athletes needed guidance not only in techniques but in mental toughness. Jigjidsuren was the kind of mentor who knew when to push his students to their limits and when to show compassion. Under his leadership, many Mongolian athletes first tasted international success. His emphasis on discipline, respect for the opponent, and self-reflection helped his students excel both on and off the mat. His role went far beyond teaching techniques; he was shaping future champions, instilling in them the values of Judo that would serve them throughout their lives.

It wasn't just the physical training that made Jigjidsuren's mentorship so impactful. He emphasized the importance of mental preparation, something that many young athletes often overlook. "A true champion," he would say, "is one who wins within their own mind before stepping onto the mat." This mindset was revolutionary for many of his students, who came from a culture where physical strength and endurance were often prioritized over mental resilience. By combining physical training with mental fortitude, Jigjidsuren helped create athletes who were not only skilled but unshakable in the face of pressure.

But no athlete can reach the heights of success alone. Alongside Jigjidsuren were many other mentors who dedicated their lives to guiding the next generation of Judo champions. These coaches were often former athletes themselves, people who had faced the same challenges their students were now encountering. They understood the hardships and the sacrifices, and they made it their mission to pass on the lessons they had learned. Their stories were woven into the fabric of Mongolia's Judo culture, and each generation of athletes had its own set of mentors who continued to build on the legacy of those before them.

The mentorship in Mongolia went beyond the traditional coaching style seen in many other countries. It was a deeply personal bond, built on trust and mutual respect. The relationship between coach and student was often one of family, with coaches taking a keen interest in the personal lives of their athletes. They were not just teaching Judo—they were shaping the character of young individuals who would one day go on to lead their communities. This sense of duty and responsibility to the athlete was what set Mongolian Judo mentors apart from others.

The importance of mentorship is particularly clear when you look at some of Mongolia's greatest Judo champions. Athletes like Mönkh-Erdene, who rose to prominence on the international stage, were products of these strong mentor relationships. Mönkh-Erdene's success in global competitions didn't come overnight. It was the culmination of years of hard work, often under the watchful eyes of dedicated mentors who knew exactly how to push him at just the right moments.

Mongolia's Judo coaches didn't just focus on preparing athletes for the next match—they were preparing them for life. They knew that the pressures of competition, the stress of representing one's country, could be overwhelming. So, they taught their athletes how to manage these challenges, how to stay focused in the face of adversity. In many ways, the Judo dojo became a place of spiritual growth, where the lessons of the mat were applied to the challenges of life outside.

The bond between coach and athlete is something that transcends the sport itself. It's about instilling values that go beyond winning medals. In Mongolia, Judo's growth has been marked not just by the success of individual athletes but by the relationship between mentors and their students—a relationship based on respect, trust, and the shared goal of becoming the best version of oneself.

As the sport continues to evolve in Mongolia, the role of the mentor remains as crucial as ever. Today's athletes still rely on the wisdom of their coaches, just as athletes did decades ago. Whether it's learning new techniques or finding the mental toughness to overcome challenges, the guidance of a coach is always at the heart of an athlete's success. The legacy of these mentors lives on in every Judo athlete who steps onto the mat, ready to face the world with the lessons they have learned and the strength they have gained.

In the end, the success of Mongolia's Judo is not just a testament to the strength of its athletes, but to the enduring power of mentorship. These coaches, through their dedication and wisdom, have transformed the lives of many young people, shaping them into champions not only in sport but in life. Their influence is felt in every match, in every victory, and in every moment of growth. They are the unsung heroes of Mongolia's Judo journey, and their legacy will continue to inspire generations to come.

How coaches blend wrestling traditions with Judo training methods.

In Mongolia, where wrestling has deep historical and cultural roots, the role of coaches in blending traditional Mongolian wrestling with Judo training methods has been pivotal in the country's success on the international Judo scene. This fusion of two distinct martial arts might seem unlikely at first, but it has been a natural evolution—one that draws from the strengths of both disciplines to produce versatile and well-rounded athletes.

Wrestling, particularly the Mongolian style known as *Bökh*, is a powerful and dynamic sport that places a significant emphasis on physical strength, balance, and technique. In Mongolian culture, wrestling is more than just a sport; it is a symbol of pride, and it is woven into the fabric of the nation's identity. The Mongolian wrestling tradition is known for its deep understanding of leverage, control, and the ability to read an opponent's movements. Unlike many other wrestling styles, which may focus heavily on pure power or endurance, Mongolian wrestling also prioritizes a sense of timing and strategy. These elements—balance, leverage, timing, and control—are the very same qualities that make Judo so effective.

Judo, although introduced relatively late to Mongolia compared to wrestling, has been embraced for its emphasis on technique and its philosophical foundations. Judo's principle of using an opponent's force against them, the idea of *maximum efficiency with minimum effort*, resonates well with the Mongolian approach to combat. Judo's throws, sweeps, and grip strategies are rooted in understanding balance and applying pressure at the right moments—much like *Bökh* wrestling, where the key to a successful throw lies in knowing when and how to use the opponent's energy to gain leverage.

Mongolian coaches have been instrumental in merging these two martial arts, integrating the strengths of traditional wrestling with Judo's technical focus. They recognize that wrestling, particularly the Mongolian style, offers a unique set of physical attributes that can benefit Judo practitioners. The explosive strength, low center of gravity, and gripping techniques developed in *Bökh* wrestling are invaluable when combined with Judo's ground techniques and tactical throwing methods.

Coaches often begin by focusing on the similarities between the two arts. Both Judo and Mongolian wrestling require athletes to maintain excellent posture and balance. In Judo, a practitioner's stance must be solid, able to absorb or redirect the opponent's energy. In *Bökh*, the wrestler's stance is similar, focusing on low positioning and using the legs to generate power. By teaching Judo athletes the low, powerful stances of wrestling, Mongolian coaches help them develop the kind of foundational strength and stability needed for effective throws in Judo.

Mongolian wrestling also emphasizes an intimate understanding of grips, particularly the grip on the opponent's arms, neck, or waist. This principle is seamlessly transferred to Judo, where grips are vital to executing effective throws. In both arts, knowing how to control the opponent's body through gripping, breaking their posture, and creating openings is key to success. Coaches have worked hard to adapt these techniques from *Bökh* into Judo's specific grip strategies, teaching athletes to move fluidly between the two styles depending on the situation.

Additionally, the mental approach that Mongolian wrestling instills is also crucial to success in Judo. In *Bökh*, the emphasis on timing, patience, and reading the opponent's intentions helps athletes develop a keen sense of situational awareness. This is incredibly valuable in Judo, where matches are often decided by split-second decisions. Coaches who blend the mental aspects of wrestling with the strategic thinking required in Judo prepare their athletes to think quickly, stay calm under pressure, and make precise decisions in the heat of competition.

Another area where the fusion of wrestling and Judo techniques proves beneficial is in the groundwork. While Judo has a distinct ground fighting element known as *ne-waza*, Mongolian wrestling doesn't focus as heavily on ground control. However, the principles of control, leverage, and balance learned in *Bökh* have given Mongolian Judo athletes a unique advantage on the ground. The wrestling focus on pinning an opponent down, controlling their movements, and forcing them into uncomfortable positions feeds directly into Judo's groundwork techniques. Coaches blend these skills, teaching Judo athletes how to combine wrestling's pressure on the ground with Judo's submission and pinning strategies.

Moreover, Mongolian coaches understand the importance of blending physical conditioning with technical training. Wrestling requires intense conditioning to develop strength and endurance, but Judo demands agility, flexibility, and fluidity. To produce well-rounded athletes, coaches focus on training methods that improve cardiovascular fitness, flexibility, strength, and explosive power—all while ensuring that their athletes maintain the fluidity and precision needed for Judo techniques. In the gym, coaches incorporate wrestling drills, such as those used to develop explosive takedowns, alongside Judo-specific exercises that improve balance, timing, and the application of technique.

A key advantage of combining these two fighting styles is the versatility it provides to the athlete. Judo's emphasis on throws, sweeps, and counters becomes even more effective when paired with the solid foundation of Mongolian wrestling's physical conditioning and tactical approach. For example, a Judo athlete trained in Mongolian wrestling might find it easier to stay low to the ground when trying to defend against a throw or to maintain control in situations where others might struggle to keep their balance. This blend allows athletes to take advantage of their opponent's weaknesses, whether standing or on the ground, using a mix of Judo's finesse and wrestling's brute strength.

The integration of *Bökh* wrestling and Judo training methods hasn't just created stronger athletes; it's helped shift the mentality of Mongolian martial artists. By combining two distinct disciplines, athletes gain a broader understanding of combat, learning how to adapt their approach based on their opponent's style and the circumstances of the match. Coaches often emphasize the importance of flexibility—not just in terms of technique, but in mindset. A wrestler might prefer direct confrontation, while a Judo player might favor a more defensive approach; the combination of both philosophies creates a more adaptable athlete, able to switch between aggressive and defensive tactics seamlessly.

Ultimately, it's the guidance of the coaches that makes this fusion successful. They are the architects of this synthesis, understanding that both wrestling and Judo have unique strengths that can complement each other. It's not just about teaching athletes to perform better in competitions; it's about teaching them to think differently, to approach each challenge with a diverse skill set, and to become more adaptable and resilient athletes in the process. The blending of Mongolian wrestling with Judo training methods has produced some of the world's most formidable martial artists, and this tradition of innovation and adaptation continues to shape the future of Judo in Mongolia.

Judo as a symbol of national identity and pride

Judo has become more than just a sport in Mongolia; it has evolved into a powerful symbol of national identity and pride. The story of how Judo, a martial art introduced from Japan, intertwined with Mongolia's cultural fabric is both remarkable and inspiring. Over the years, Judo has become a defining part of the country's sporting legacy, reflecting the resilience, discipline, and strength that the Mongolian people hold dear.

Mongolia has a rich history of wrestling, an ancient tradition that predates Judo. Wrestling, particularly Bökh, is woven into the very fabric of Mongolian culture, revered as the ultimate display of strength and skill. When Judo was introduced to the country, it was seen as something foreign, something different. It wasn't particularly embraced by everyone; in fact, some even viewed it with skepticism. Yet, over time, something incredible happened—Judo began to capture the imagination of the Mongolian people, and soon, it wasn't just another sport. It became a representation of the nation's strength and resilience on the global stage.

In Mongolia, sports are never just about the physical act of the game itself. Sports are a reflection of the national spirit, of the qualities that define the country's character. The people of Mongolia

Chapter 12: Judo's Cultural Impact in Mongolia

Judo as a symbol of national identity and pride.

Judo has become more than just a sport in Mongolia; it has evolved into a powerful symbol of national identity and pride. The story of how Judo, a martial art introduced from Japan, intertwined with Mongolia's cultural fabric is both remarkable and inspiring. Over the years, Judo has become a defining part of the country's sporting legacy, reflecting the resilience, discipline, and strength that the Mongolian people hold dear.

Mongolia has a rich history of wrestling, an ancient tradition that predates Judo. Wrestling, particularly *Bökh*, is woven into the very fabric of Mongolian culture, revered as the ultimate display of strength and skill. When Judo was introduced to the country, it was seen as something foreign, something different. It wasn't immediately embraced by everyone; in fact, some even viewed it with skepticism. Yet, over time, something incredible happened—Judo began to capture the imagination of the Mongolian people, and soon, it wasn't just another sport. It became a representation of the nation's strength and resilience on the global stage.

In Mongolia, sports are never just about the individual athlete or the game itself. Sports are a reflection of the national spirit, of the qualities that define the country's character. The people of Mongolia take immense pride in their warriors, their fighters, their champions. So, when Judo began to produce international champions, it quickly became a source of national pride. These athletes were not just winning medals; they were symbolizing the very essence of Mongolia's warrior spirit. Judo's rise in Mongolia wasn't just a victory for the athletes themselves; it was a triumph for the entire nation. Every medal won, every victory achieved, added to the collective pride of a country that had long been proud of its martial heritage.

The cultural shift was gradual, but undeniable. As Judo gained popularity, it began to be seen through the lens of Mongolian values. The discipline, respect, and perseverance inherent in Judo meshed well with the qualities that Mongolian culture had long prized. *Bökh* wrestling, with its focus on technique, balance, and control, shares many commonalities with Judo. Both sports require not just physical strength but mental fortitude. This overlap allowed Judo to be embraced more readily by the Mongolian people, who began to see it as an extension of their own traditions. As Mongolian athletes competed and won on the world stage, Judo started to represent not just the success of individual athletes, but the strength of the nation as a whole.

Judo's role in shaping Mongolian national identity became more apparent as the years went by. The international success of Mongolian

Judo athletes, particularly in major tournaments like the World Judo Championships and the Olympic Games, created a sense of unity and pride among the people. These athletes weren't just representing themselves—they were representing Mongolia, its culture, and its values. In the midst of a rapidly changing world, where globalization was altering the traditional cultural landscape, Judo offered Mongolia a way to assert its place on the global stage, while staying true to its roots.

The Mongolian people began to see Judo as a symbol of their nation's growing prominence in the world. The victories of athletes like Tuvshinbayar Naidan, who won Mongolia's first Olympic gold in Judo in 2008, became a moment of national celebration. The moment he stood on that podium, the Mongolian flag raised high above him, was not just a victory for Tuvshinbayar—it was a victory for every Mongolian who believed in the potential of their country. It was a reminder that, despite being a small nation with a challenging history, Mongolia could compete on the world stage and win.

As Judo's influence grew, it also started to shape the country's youth. The success of the national Judo team inspired a new generation of Mongolian athletes, eager to prove themselves on the mat and in the world. In rural villages and urban centers alike, young people began to flock to Judo dojos, eager to embrace a discipline that not only taught them how to fight but also instilled in them a sense of respect, honor, and self-control. These young athletes viewed Judo not just as a sport, but as a way to carry on the proud traditions of their ancestors, who valued strength and honor above all else.

Judo's cultural impact also extended beyond the realm of sports. It began to influence Mongolia's broader cultural landscape. The values of respect, humility, and self-discipline—core to Judo philosophy—started to resonate more widely within Mongolian society. In a world where material success and individualism often take center stage, Judo's focus on the importance of collective effort, mutual respect, and personal growth offered a refreshing alternative. It became a framework for how people should live their lives, not just how they should fight.

The rise of Judo in Mongolia also mirrored the country's transition in the modern world. After decades of Soviet influence, Mongolia had entered a new era, seeking to assert its independence and cultural identity. Judo, with its emphasis on strategy, mental resilience, and physical prowess, became a symbol of this new Mongolian identity. It represented the country's ability to adapt, to modernize, while still holding onto the traditional values that had long defined its culture. It was a sport that bridged the gap between the old and the new, between tradition and progress.

As Judo continued to thrive in Mongolia, it became clear that it was no longer just a foreign sport—it had become an integral part of

Mongolian life. The victories on the international stage were more than just athletic achievements; they were moments of national reflection and pride. They were reminders that Mongolia, with its rich history, its resilient people, and its proud warrior spirit, had a place in the world. Judo had become a lens through which the world saw Mongolia, and through which the Mongolian people saw themselves.

In the end, Judo's cultural impact in Mongolia cannot be measured simply by the medals won or the victories achieved. It is about the values it has instilled in the nation—the respect for tradition, the pursuit of excellence, and the belief in the strength of the individual and the community. Judo has become a symbol of Mongolia's identity, an embodiment of its history, its culture, and its place in the world. It is a sport that will continue to inspire generations of Mongolians to come, instilling in them the same pride and determination that has defined the nation for centuries.

Chapter 13: Overcoming Challenges in Sports Development

Mongolia's journey in the world of sports, particularly in Judo, has been a path filled with both triumph and struggle. Despite the growing success of its athletes, there are still significant hurdles that the country faces when it comes to the infrastructure and economic support needed to build a sustainable sporting culture. The story of Mongolian sports is not just one of passion and skill; it is also about the struggle to overcome resource limitations, lack of proper facilities, and the ongoing effort to attract sponsorships that can provide the necessary funding for the athletes.

One of the biggest challenges has always been the lack of funding and proper infrastructure. The economic conditions in Mongolia, a country that has historically been reliant on its pastoral economy, have made it difficult to invest large sums into sports development. While the country has produced world-class athletes in several disciplines, including Judo, the facilities needed for training, competing, and nurturing future stars have not always been up to par. Training centers are often outdated, and the equipment available to athletes may not always meet international standards. For a nation looking to compete with the global powers in sports, this gap in resources is a major obstacle.

Take Judo, for example. Despite the incredible achievements of Mongolian athletes on the international stage, many of these athletes have had to train in less-than-ideal conditions. They often make do with what they have, relying more on their determination, discipline, and the knowledge of their coaches than on the luxury of state-of-the-art gyms or top-notch facilities. Many of the dojos across Mongolia, particularly in rural areas, lack the proper space, equipment, and training staff needed to take an athlete from a local level to an international one. Yet, despite these limitations, the athletes' spirit remains unbroken. They continue to train under harsh conditions because of their love for the sport and their deep desire to represent Mongolia on the world stage.

However, the government of Mongolia, alongside private sponsors, has started to take notice. The country has made strides in recent years to improve its sports infrastructure, especially in Judo. Recognizing the impact that sports success has on national pride, there has been a renewed push to build better training facilities and invest in coaching programs. The government, which has long been involved in promoting sports, particularly after the country's transition from Soviet influence, has started to allocate more funds for sports development. New sports complexes, gyms, and training centers have been constructed, and existing ones have been renovated to accommodate the growing number of athletes. These investments, though still relatively small in comparison to those in wealthier nations, represent a positive shift towards more sustainable growth for Mongolian sports.

The private sector has also begun to play a more significant role. Sponsorships from businesses and corporations, both local and international, have become more common in recent years. While the amount of money flowing into Mongolian sports is still far less than what is seen in more developed countries, it's a step in the right direction. Companies see the value in associating their brand with successful athletes, especially when those athletes represent Mongolia's strength, resilience, and rich history. These partnerships, though modest, have provided much-needed financial support to the Judo community, helping fund athlete training, international competitions, and even the construction of new facilities.

What's been most exciting, however, is the creation of specialized programs aimed at developing Judo talent from a young age. The government, in collaboration with various sports organizations, has started to put more emphasis on youth development. Training programs that target young people from all over the country are being set up. The aim is to identify promising athletes early and provide them with the coaching, facilities, and support they need to reach the highest levels of competition. The concept of nurturing young talent from rural areas, where Judo has traditionally not been as popular, is also gaining ground. These youth programs are offering scholarships, providing access to better training, and making sure that talented athletes don't miss out on the opportunity to compete at the national or international level simply because they come from a less privileged background.

As these initiatives gain traction, there is hope that the next generation of Mongolian Judo stars will have the tools and opportunities that their predecessors lacked. The country is building a pipeline of talent that is better prepared for international success, and with the backing of improved facilities and coaching programs, the future looks bright for Judo in Mongolia.

In the heart of this transformation is the growing awareness of how important it is for Mongolia to not just be proud of its champions, but to invest in creating more champions. These investments in infrastructure and youth development programs are a clear indication that Mongolia is serious about developing sports, and particularly Judo, into a cornerstone of national pride. However, the challenges remain. The resources are still limited, and the road ahead is long. But there is a sense of optimism. As athletes continue to rise through the ranks, competing at world-class levels, and as sponsorships and government investments increase, the future of Judo in Mongolia will likely mirror the nation's progress—rising steadily despite the obstacles.

For many of the athletes, this growing support is a beacon of hope. They no longer have to train in underfunded dojos or struggle to find the resources they need to compete internationally. The vision for the future is clear: a generation of Mongolian athletes, properly equipped and supported, competing not just with heart, but with the tools to win. Judo has become more than just a sport for these athletes—it has become a way of life, a path to honor their country and inspire others to follow in their footsteps. With each step forward in infrastructure and support, Mongolia gets closer to realizing its dream of becoming a true powerhouse in Judo and other sports on the global stage.

Chapter 13: Overcoming Challenges in Sports Development

Mongolia's journey in the world of sports, particularly in Judo, has been a path filled with both triumph and struggle. Despite the growing success of its athletes, there are still significant hurdles that the country faces when it comes to the infrastructure and economic support needed to build a sustainable sporting culture. The story of Mongolian sports is not just one of passion and skill; it is also about the struggle to overcome resource limitations, lack of proper facilities, and the ongoing effort to attract sponsorships that can provide the necessary funding for the athletes.

One of the biggest challenges has always been the lack of funding and proper infrastructure. The economic conditions in Mongolia, a country that has historically been reliant on its pastoral economy, have made it difficult to invest large sums into sports development. While the country has produced world-class athletes in several disciplines, including Judo, the facilities needed for training, competing, and nurturing future stars have not always been up to par. Training centers are often outdated, and the equipment available to athletes may not always meet international standards. For a nation looking to compete with the global powers in sports, this gap in resources is a major obstacle.

Take Judo, for example. Despite the incredible achievements of Mongolian athletes on the international stage, many of these athletes have had to train in less-than-ideal conditions. They often make do with what they have, relying more on their determination, discipline, and the knowledge of their coaches than on the luxury of state-of-the-art gyms or top-notch facilities. Many of the dojos across Mongolia, particularly in rural areas, lack the proper space, equipment, and training staff needed to take an athlete from a local level to an international one. Yet, despite these limitations, the athletes' spirit remains unbroken. They continue to train under harsh conditions because of their love for the sport and their deep desire to represent Mongolia on the world stage.

However, the government of Mongolia, alongside private sponsors, has started to take notice. The country has made strides in recent years to improve its sports infrastructure, especially in Judo. Recognizing the impact that sports success has on national pride, there has been a renewed push to build better training facilities and invest in coaching programs. The government, which has long been involved in promoting sports, particularly after the country's transition from Soviet influence, has started to allocate more funds for sports development. New sports complexes, gyms, and training centers have been constructed, and existing ones have been renovated to accommodate the growing number of athletes. These investments, though still relatively small in comparison to those in wealthier nations, represent a positive shift towards more sustainable growth for Mongolian sports.

The private sector has also begun to play a more significant role. Sponsorships from businesses and corporations, both local and international, have become more common in recent years. While the amount of money flowing into Mongolian sports is still far less than what is seen in more developed countries, it's a step in the right direction. Companies see the value in associating their brand with successful athletes, especially when those athletes represent Mongolia's strength, resilience, and rich history. These partnerships, though modest, have provided much-needed financial support to the Judo community, helping fund athlete training, international competitions, and even the construction of new facilities.

What's been most exciting, however, is the creation of specialized programs aimed at developing Judo talent from a young age. The government, in collaboration with various sports organizations, has started to put more emphasis on youth development. Training programs that target young people from all over the country are being set up. The aim is to identify promising athletes early and provide them with the coaching, facilities, and support they need to reach the highest levels of competition. The concept of nurturing young talent from rural areas, where Judo has traditionally not been as popular, is also gaining ground. These youth programs are offering scholarships, providing access to better training, and making sure that talented athletes don't miss out on the opportunity to compete at the national or international level simply because they come from a less privileged background.

As these initiatives gain traction, there is hope that the next generation of Mongolian Judo stars will have the tools and opportunities that their predecessors lacked. The country is building a pipeline of talent that is better prepared for international success, and with the backing of improved facilities and coaching programs, the future looks bright for Judo in Mongolia.

In the heart of this transformation is the growing awareness of how important it is for Mongolia to not just be proud of its champions, but to invest in creating more champions. These investments in infrastructure and youth development programs are a clear indication that Mongolia is serious about developing sports, and particularly Judo, into a cornerstone of national pride. However, the challenges remain. The resources are still limited, and the road ahead is long. But there is a sense of optimism. As athletes continue to rise through the ranks, competing at world-class levels, and as sponsorships and government investments increase, the future of Judo in Mongolia will likely mirror the nation's progress—rising steadily despite the obstacles.

For many of the athletes, this growing support is a beacon of hope. They no longer have to train in underfunded dojos or struggle to find the resources they need to compete internationally. The vision for the future is clear: a generation of Mongolian athletes, properly equipped and supported, competing not just with heart, but with the tools to win. Judo has become more than just a sport for these athletes—it has become a way of life, a path to honor their country and inspire others to follow in their footsteps. With each step forward in infrastructure and support, Mongolia gets closer to realizing its dream of becoming a true powerhouse in Judo and other sports on the global stage.

Chapter 14: The Future of Judo in Mongolia

Mongolia's success in Judo has been nothing short of extraordinary. What started as a sport that was introduced from abroad has transformed into a powerful force on the international scene, giving the country a place among the world's top contenders. As Mongolia continues to make strides in Judo, there is a clear potential for the country to not only maintain its position but to further solidify its dominance. The athletes, the coaches, and the entire sports community have created a foundation that could carry Mongolia's Judo legacy well into the future. But for that to happen, the country will need to embrace the challenges ahead, develop new talents, and create a sustainable system that nurtures champions.

When you look at the history of Mongolia's success in Judo, it's easy to see why the future looks promising. Athletes like Tuvshinbayar Naidan, who captured Mongolia's first Olympic gold in Judo in 2008, set the stage for the country's rise on the global stage. His victory was a breakthrough moment that not only showcased Mongolia's prowess in the sport but also inspired a new generation of athletes. Since then, there have been several notable Mongolian Judo competitors, each contributing to the growing recognition of the country in the sport. These victories didn't just bring home medals; they elevated the nation's pride, demonstrating that with the right mentality, skill, and determination, even a small country like Mongolia could make its mark in the world.

But the true potential for Mongolia's continued dominance lies in its emerging talents. In every corner of the country, from the bustling capital of Ulaanbaatar to the quiet, remote villages, young athletes are beginning to step up. These future champions are more than just hopefuls; they are a reflection of the country's rich martial heritage, a testament to the values of discipline, respect, and hard work that the Mongolian people hold dear.

Among these emerging talents, there are a few names that stand out. Young athletes, some still in their teens, are showing promise with their performances on the junior circuit. Their technique, mental toughness, and hunger for success are evident every time they step onto the mat. These athletes have the potential to follow in the footsteps of their predecessors, but they also bring new skills and strategies that could elevate Mongolia's presence in Judo even further. The next generation of Mongolian Judo athletes understands that the stakes are high, and they are ready to continue the work of their predecessors, pushing the boundaries and setting new records.

To ensure that these emerging talents realize their full potential, it's essential for the country to continue investing in its sports infrastructure and development programs. The foundation has been laid, but the key to sustaining success lies in the ability to cultivate future champions. Programs that identify and nurture young athletes from an early age are already in place, but they must be expanded and improved. Access to better training facilities, top-tier coaching, and international exposure is crucial. Many of Mongolia's top athletes have achieved success despite the challenges of limited resources, but to continue competing at the highest level, the next generation needs the tools to succeed.

One of the main strategies for sustaining success is ensuring that the country's best Judo athletes have the right mentorship and support. The role of the coach is critical in shaping the future of any athlete, and in Mongolia, there are seasoned mentors who have seen the sport grow and evolve. These coaches are more than just trainers—they are leaders who guide the athletes through the mental and physical challenges of Judo. They instill in them not only the techniques necessary to win but also the mindset to deal with setbacks, the patience to stay disciplined, and the resilience to face adversity. By continuing to invest in the development of these coaches, Mongolia will ensure that its athletes receive the best guidance and training available.

Another strategy for continued success is creating a stronger network for international competition. Mongolian athletes already excel on the world stage, but to maintain this level of excellence, there must be more opportunities for exposure to the best in the world. Training camps, international tournaments, and exchanges with other Judo powerhouses will help Mongolian athletes hone their skills and adapt to different styles of competition. While many of the country's athletes have trained primarily in Mongolia, international experiences are vital for developing a well-rounded and adaptable fighter.

Furthermore, it's important to foster a culture of Judo not just in the cities but in rural areas as well. This will require outreach programs that introduce the sport to younger generations who might not have easy access to formal training facilities. Many of Mongolia's most successful athletes have come from humble backgrounds, where resources were scarce, and their journey was one of sheer determination and grit. If more kids from rural parts of the country are given the opportunity to train in Judo, the talent pool will continue to grow, and the nation will have a more diverse group of athletes to draw from.

The role of private sponsorships and government funding will also be crucial in ensuring that Mongolia's Judo program continues to thrive. While the government has started to invest more in sports, including Judo, it must continue to prioritize these investments, not just in the form of new facilities but also in terms of providing athletes with scholarships, training grants, and other forms of support. The private sector has an important part to play as well, with businesses needing to recognize the value of supporting Judo as a national sport. Sponsorships not only provide financial backing but also increase the visibility of the sport, helping to build its following both domestically and internationally.

The key to Mongolia's continued dominance in Judo will be a combination of factors: infrastructure, mentorship, international exposure, and a strong commitment to youth development. The country has already proven that it has the talent and the spirit to compete with the best, but the future will depend on how well these resources are managed and expanded. If Mongolia continues to nurture its athletes, build better facilities, and secure the support they need, there is no doubt that the next generation of Judo stars will rise to even greater heights.

Mongolia has proven time and again that it has what it takes to compete on the global stage, and with the emerging talent in the ranks, the future of Judo in Mongolia is bright. The country's legacy in Judo is far from finished; it is only just beginning. The next few decades could very well see Mongolia emerge as a dominant force in Judo, continuing to inspire not just its own people but the world as a whole.

Conclusion

A Legacy of Strength and Honor

Mongolia's journey in Judo has been a tale of resilience, grit, and unwavering determination. It's a story rooted deeply in the country's history, culture, and values. From the vast steppes of Mongolia to the competitive arenas of the world, the athletes who have risen to prominence in this sport have carried with them the weight of a nation's pride. They have embodied the strength and honor that are synonymous with Mongolia's identity, and through their victories, they've written a legacy that will be remembered for generations to come.

When you look at the history of Mongolian Judo, it's clear that it's not just a sport; it's a reflection of the very spirit of the people. For a nation that has always lived by the principles of courage, respect, and hard work, Judo has become more than just a way to win medals. It has become a symbol of what it means to be Mongolian—resilient in the face of adversity, proud of its heritage, and relentless in the pursuit of excellence. These values are not just instilled in athletes but are deeply ingrained in the entire culture of Mongolia. The perseverance to succeed, no matter the circumstances, is a lesson taught to children from an early age, and it's this perseverance that has made Mongolian Judo so powerful on the world stage.

The athletes who have represented Mongolia in Judo, from the legendary Tuvshinbayar Naidan to the emerging stars who carry the hopes of the next generation, have each contributed to a legacy that will outlive them. Their success is not just about personal achievement; it's about national pride. Every medal won, every victory celebrated, serves as a testament to what can be achieved through hard work and determination. And perhaps even more importantly, it serves as an inspiration to the young athletes who look up to them and dream of one day stepping onto that same international stage. These champions have become symbols of hope and possibility, showing the world that a small nation with a big heart can compete with the best.

But Judo's impact in Mongolia extends beyond just the athletes. It has become a part of the national consciousness. When a Mongolian athlete steps onto the mat, they're not just representing themselves—they're representing their families, their communities, and the entire nation. The sport has become a unifying force, bringing the country together in ways that few other things can. The victories, the moments of glory, are celebrated not just in the gym or the arena, but in every corner of Mongolia. From the most remote village to the heart of Ulaanbaatar, the pride of the nation swells with each win, and the collective joy is felt throughout the land. It's a celebration of identity, a celebration of what it means to be Mongolian, and it's something that transcends the individual.

As Mongolia looks to the future, the question remains: how will the country sustain and build upon this legacy? The challenges are clear. The infrastructure is still developing, and resources are limited, but the foundation has been laid. The athletes of tomorrow have a stronger platform than ever before, with better access to training facilities, international exposure, and the unwavering support of their country. And with the current emphasis on youth development, the future of Mongolian Judo looks brighter than ever.

The young athletes emerging from every corner of Mongolia are the ones who will carry the torch forward. They will face challenges that their predecessors could only dream of, but they will also have the tools and the support to overcome them. With the country's renewed focus on building better facilities, providing better training, and securing sponsorships, there is little doubt that Mongolia's Judo scene will continue to grow. The athletes of tomorrow will not just compete; they will dominate. They will build on the legacy that has been left for them, and they will create a new chapter in the history of Mongolian Judo that will inspire the world.

But it's not just about the medals or the victories. It's about something deeper. Judo teaches discipline, humility, and respect—values that are essential for the individual and for society as a whole. These are the values that are passed down through generations, the values that are woven into the very fabric of Mongolia's culture. As long as Judo remains a part of the national identity, it will continue to shape the character of the people, building strength not only in the body but in the spirit. And it will continue to serve as a powerful reminder of what can be achieved when a people are united by a common goal.

Mongolia's legacy in Judo is not just a story of triumph—it is a story of honor, strength, and a profound connection to the land and the culture that shapes its people. It is a legacy that will endure for generations to come, inspiring future champions to rise up and carry the flag of Mongolia high on the world stage. And as long as the spirit of Judo remains in the hearts of the people, that legacy will never fade. It will continue to grow, evolve, and inspire, much like the country itself—strong, proud, and ever-reaching for greatness.

Appendix A: Timeline of Key Events in Mongolian Judo History

- **1960s-1970s:** The introduction of Judo in Mongolia. Early exposure to the sport through Japanese missionaries and cultural exchanges with the Soviet Union. Initial training efforts begin, and Mongolia starts developing its first Judo athletes.

- **1980s:** Mongolia's first Judo competition at the national level. The sport starts gaining popularity among young athletes, especially in Ulaanbaatar, where Judo clubs are established. The first batch of Mongolian athletes begins competing in international tournaments.

- **1990:** Mongolia becomes a member of the International Judo Federation (IJF), marking an important step for the country's formal entry into the global Judo community.

- **2000:** The Mongolian Judo Federation is officially established. The country's Judo program becomes more structured with the development of national training programs.

- **2008:** Tuvshinbayar Naidan wins Mongolia's first Olympic gold in Judo at the Beijing Olympics. His victory is a landmark achievement and brings national pride and recognition to Mongolia's Judo program.

- **2012:** Mongolia continues to build on the success of 2008, with several athletes earning medals at the World Judo Championships and the London Olympics. The country solidifies its position as a Judo power in Asia.

- **2016:** Mongolia earns several medals in the Rio Olympics. The country's success continues to inspire the next generation of Judo athletes. A surge in youth participation in Judo begins to reshape Mongolia's sports landscape.

- **2020-2021:** Despite the COVID-19 pandemic, Mongolia maintains its commitment to developing Judo, with athletes continuing training under strict protocols. The Mongolian Judo Federation pushes for more sponsorships and infrastructure development.

- **2024 and Beyond:** The next generation of Mongolian Judo athletes begins to emerge as top contenders in international competitions. Mongolia is poised to further cement its position as a powerhouse in the global Judo scene.

Appendix B: Profiles of Notable Mongolian Judo Champions

1. **Tuvshinbayar Naidan**

   - **Born:** 1984, Ulaanbaatar, Mongolia
   - **Key Achievements:**
     - Olympic Gold Medalist (2008, Beijing)
     - World Judo Champion (2010, Tokyo)
     - Multiple Asian Championship medals
   - **Legacy:** Tuvshinbayar Naidan's victory at the 2008 Olympics marked a historic moment for Mongolia, bringing the first-ever Olympic gold in Judo to the country. His success has inspired a new generation of Judo athletes, and he remains a national hero.

2. **Munkhbat's Sumiya**

   - **Born:** 1984, Mongolia
   - **Key Achievements:**
     - Olympic Bronze Medalist (2012, London)
     - World Judo Championships Silver Medalist (2011, Paris)
   - **Legacy:** Munkhbat Sumiya's bronze medal in London made her the first Mongolian woman to earn an Olympic medal in Judo. She has paved the way for

more female athletes in Judo and remains a trailblazer in Mongolia's sporting history.

3. **Odbayar Ganbaatar**

   o **Born:** 1991, Mongolia
   o **Key Achievements:**
      ▪ Asian Judo Champion (2018)
      ▪ World Judo Championships Bronze Medalist (2017, Budapest)
   o **Legacy:** Odbayar Ganbaatar has been a consistent performer on the international circuit, earning multiple podium finishes in major championships. His drive and commitment have made him a key figure in the evolution of Mongolian Judo.

4. **Bolormaa Tserendorj**

   o **Born:** 1987, Ulaanbaatar, Mongolia
   o **Key Achievements:**
      ▪ Asian Judo Championships Gold Medalist (2016)
      ▪ Multiple IJF World Tour medals
   o **Legacy:** Bolormaa has been one of Mongolia's leading female Judo athletes. Her success has provided

inspiration to young girls in the country, encouraging greater female participation in the sport.

Appendix C: Traditional Bökh Wrestling Techniques Adapted to Judo

1. **Khuushu (Body Throw)**

   o   In Bökh, the Khuushu involves gripping the opponent's body and throwing them off balance. In Judo, this technique is adapted into various grips such as the *seoi-nage* (shoulder throw) and *harai-goshi* (hip throw). The emphasis in both traditions is on timing and leverage rather than brute strength.

2. **Shuvuun (Sweeping the Legs)**

   o   The Shuvuun technique in Bökh focuses on sweeping the opponent's legs to trip them. In Judo, a similar technique is *de-ashi-barai* (major foot sweep), where an athlete uses their foot to trip an opponent, often combined with a push to destabilize them.

3. **Togtokh (Leg Grabs)**

   o   In Bökh, athletes frequently use leg grabs to control their opponent. This technique has been adapted in Judo through *kouchi-gari* (minor inner reaping) and *osoto-gari* (major outer reaping), where the focus is on destabilizing the opponent's stance and executing a clean throw.

4. **Kherlen (Counterbalance and Grip)**

   ○ The Kherlen technique in Bökh is used to gain control by manipulating the opponent's body weight, forcing them off balance. This concept is mirrored in Judo by various grips and counterattacks that aim to break an opponent's posture and create openings for throws.

Appendix D: Judo Training Drills Inspired by Bökh Wrestling

1. **Footwork Drills (Bökh-Inspired)**

   ○ In Bökh, wrestlers practice a lot of footwork to shift their weight and maintain stability. Judo athletes adapt these drills to develop quick, explosive movement on the mat, practicing *ashiwaza* (foot techniques) with a focus on fluid transitions between steps, mimicking the fast foot changes seen in traditional wrestling.

2. **Takedown Practice**

- ○ Bökh emphasizes powerful takedowns, and Judo athletes replicate these with drills that focus on lifting and throwing the opponent to the ground. One common drill includes practicing *uchi-mata* (inner thigh throw) while maintaining strong posture, akin to the wrestling techniques used to drive opponents to the mat in Bökh.

3. **Grip and Control Drills**

- ○ In both Bökh and Judo, strong grips and control of the opponent's body are crucial. In Judo, *kata-gatame* (shoulder hold) and *ne-waza* (ground techniques) often incorporate grips that are inspired by traditional wrestling holds, emphasizing control and balance while attempting to execute throws or pins.

4. **Counter-Technique Drills**

- ○ Wrestling's emphasis on counters translates directly into Judo, where counter techniques (such as *tai-otoshi* or *sumi-gaeshi*) are trained by practicing against simulated attacks. These drills focus on using an opponent's momentum to gain leverage and execute throws, much like in Bökh where counters are critical for success.

Author Bio
Leighton Antonio Shepherd

Author Bio:
Leighton Tokunbo Shepherd

Leighton Tokunbo Shepherd is a 67-year-old martial artist and teacher who has dedicated over five decades of his life to Judo. Based in Beijing, China, where he's lived most of his life, Shepherd's passion for Judo began as a young man when he first stepped into a small dojo and fell in love with its balance of strength, strategy, and discipline.

Shepherd isn't just someone who practices Judo—he lives it. Over the years, he's competed, taught, and mentored countless students, always focusing on the deeper lessons behind the techniques. To him, Judo is more than a martial art; it's a way of facing life's challenges with confidence and adaptability.

In addition to his work on the mat, Shepherd has spent years reflecting on how the principles of Judo apply to life outside the dojo. Through his teaching and writing, he shares how anyone—whether they practice Judo or not—can benefit from its lessons in resilience, balance, and self-discovery.

Now semi-retired, Shepherd continues to teach in Beijing and is a respected voice in the martial arts community. His straightforward, relatable style makes his insights accessible to everyone, whether they're seasoned martial artists or complete beginners.

From Falling to Flying is his way of sharing what Judo has taught him over a lifetime—about falling, adapting, and thriving, not just in Judo but in life itself.

Made in the USA
Monee, IL
11 February 2025

12062998R00115